The School of Christian Perfection

PERMISSU SUPERIORUM C.SS.R.
NIHIL OBSTAT:
Patrick J. Supple
Censor Librorum
IMPRIMATUR:
+William Cardinal O'Connell
Archbishop of Boston

THE SCHOOL OF CHRISTIAN PERFECTION

St. Alphonsus Liguori

Translated by
Cornelius J. Warren

TAN Books
Gastonia, North Carolina

This edition of *The School of Christian Perfection* was retypeset from the edition published by Mission Church Press, Boston, 1910, and republished in 2025 by TAN Books.

Cover design by Caroline Green

Cover image: *Saint Alphonsus Liguori* (18th century) by Anonymous/Italian School. Public domain via Wikimedia Commons.

ISBN: 978-1-5051-3557-2
Kindle ISBN: 978-1-5051-3559-6
ePUB ISBN: 978-1-5051-3558-9

Published in the United States by
TAN Books
PO Box 269
Gastonia, NC 28053
www.TANBooks.com

Printed in India

Contents

St. Alphonsus Liguori
1696–1787
Bishop, Founder of the Redemptorists,
and Doctor of the Church

St. Alphonsus Liguori

Saint Alphonsus Mary de Liguori was born in 1696 near Naples, Italy, to a noble Neopolitan family. He was the son of a captain of the royal galleys. St. Alphonsus received a doctorate in both canon and civil law at the age of sixteen, and practiced law very successfully for eight years. But he abandoned the practice of law to become a priest, being ordained in 1726.

In 1732 St. Alphonsus founded the Congregation of the Most Holy Redeemer, the Redemptorists. This order was established in the face of huge difficulties; it was even divided by a schism at the time of St. Alphonsus' death. The Redemptorists have become famous for giving "missions" to enkindle and rejuvenate souls with true religious fervor.

In 1762 St. Alphonsus was obliged to become Bishop of St. Agatha. As bishop he reformed his small but slack diocese, but chronic ill health forced him to retire and he devoted himself anew to ascetical and moral theology. His experience in a lay profession, combined with natural common sense and sweetness of disposition, helped much to make him the best known of all moral theologians.

St. Alphonsus wrote numerous books, including his Moral Theology; of his many excellent devotional works, the masterpiece entitled The Glories of Mary is the most famous. He also spent much time combating anticlericalism and the heresy of Jansenism, and he was involved in several controversies regarding probabilism.

During the last years of his life St. Alphonsus suffered from ill health, especially from rheumatism which left him partially paralyzed. He experienced the dark night of the soul for several years toward the end of his life, but this period of suffering was followed by a period of peace and light during which he experienced visions and ecstasies, performed miracles, and made prophecies that later came true.

St. Alphonsus died in 1787, within two months of his 91st birthday. He was canonized in 1839, and in 1871 Pope Pius IX declared him a Doctor of the

Church. His body rests in the church of his fathers at Pagani di Nocera.

Preface

In the ascetical writings of the holy Bishop and Doctor of the Church, St. Alphonsus de Ligouri, there is a characteristic charm and an irresistible attraction. Whoever reads them with the proper dispositions will discover in them an indefinable something that appeals to the heart and stirs it to its very depths. We imagine we see the loving personality of the holy Bishop before us, and hear the words of eternal life from his very lips. According to a beautiful legend, the visitor at the shrine of St. John at Ephesus can hear the pulsations of the Saint's heart enclosed in the tomb. The heart of Alphonsus still throbs in his ascetical writings, where the whole being of the Saint seems enshrined. Little wonder therefore that the reverence and love entertained towards him in life should have passed to his edifying works, the reflex of his very self. There are few ascetical writers more widely known and more sincerely loved than St. Alphonsus.

The present volume is made up of choice selections from the various ascetical writings of the Saint. The order of virtues considered is that followed by the spiritual sons of St. Alphonsus in the Congregation of the Most Holy Redeemer. For each month of the year is assigned a particular virtue to which they are to devote their especial attention. This is a practice highly recommended by the masters of the spiritual life, and is fraught with the happiest results. It is hoped that the faithful will derive spiritual profit and pleasure from this course in "The School of Christian Perfection."

C. J. W.

Chapter I

Faith

"I am the light of the world; he that followeth me, walketh not in darkness, but shall have the light of life."—John 8:12

Faith is a divinely infused virtue by which man believes, on God's authority, what God has revealed and teaches through His Holy Church. St. Paul calls faith "the substance of things to be hoped for, and the evidence of things that appear not." (Heb. 11:1). Faith is indeed "the substance of things to be hoped for," that is to say, the foundation of our hope, for without faith, hope could not exist. Faith is likewise an evidence of the unseen, "the evidence of things that appear not."

It is quite true that there is a bright and a dark side to the practice of holy faith. Its bright side is the marks of credibility that assure us beyond shadow of doubt that our faith is the true and only faith. Its dark side is the truths themselves which are veiled from our eyes. The proofs for the truth of our holy faith are so clear that, as Pico of Mirandola says, a man must be wholly bereft of reason to refuse them credence. "Thy testimonies, O Lord, are exceedingly credible," says the Psalmist. (Ps. 92:5). Consequently, unbelievers have no excuse for refusing to submit their reason to the teachings of our holy faith. "He who believes not, is already condemned," says our Divine Saviour. On the other hand, God has willed that the objects of our belief should remain obscure in order that, by faith, we may merit a reward. From what has been said, it follows that faith gives us knowledge which surpasses in dignity all scientific truths. "Behold," exclaims Job, "how great is our God; he exceedeth all our knowledge." (Job 36:26).

Our holy faith is a treasure of unspeakable value, for in it we possess first of all a divine light which serves to guide us safely on the way to Heaven. That which we perceive with our senses or comprehend with our reason may and often does lead us astray. The truths of faith, on the contrary, are revealed by God, who can neither deceive nor be deceived. In the second place, faith furnishes us with an excellent means of showing our reverence and respect for God.

It is no more than right that we subject to God our will by the observance of His holy law, and our reason by believing His infallible word. Were man to believe only that which he sees and understands, would he be giving honor to God thereby? Assuredly not. But we undoubtedly give honor to God when we accept as certain what God has revealed, though we may neither see nor comprehend it, and believe not because we understand but simply because God has revealed it. In the third place, faith supplies us with an abundant source of merit. If the truths proposed for our acceptance were so clear and comprehensible that we could not reasonably refuse our assent, their acceptance would in no way be meritorious, for the merit of faith consists in this, that we accept and believe the truths proposed, freely and without constraint. St. Gregory expresses this truth in the following words: "Faith loses its merit when human reason furnishes a proof." (Hom. 26). Our Blessed Saviour commends those who accept the truths of faith without being able to perceive or comprehend them: "Blessed are they that have not seen, and have believed." (John 20:29).

OUR SHIELD AND PROTECTION

Faith is, moreover, a shield of protection against the enemies of our salvation. St. John says: "This is the victory which overcometh the world, our faith." (1 John 5:4). God has created us simply to labor at our souls' salvation and to become holy. "This is the will of God, your sanctification," says the Apostle. (1 Thess. 4:3). To this end all our efforts must be directed, and faith puts us in a position to overcome all the obstacles which the world opposes to the realization of our object, obstacles such as human respect, the inordinate desires of the flesh, in a word, all the temptations of Hell. The devil is very powerful, no doubt, and his temptations are calculated to inspire us with fear and dread. But the man of faith triumphs over all his attacks. "The devil," says St. Peter (1 Peter 5:8–9), "as a roaring lion goeth about seeking whom he may devour. Whom resist ye, strong in faith." St. Paul writes in a similar strain: "In all things taking the shield of faith, wherewith you may be able to extinguish all the fiery darts of the most wicked one." (Eph. 6:16). As a shield protects the body from the arrows of an enemy, so faith defends the soul against the assaults of Hell.

"My just man liveth by faith," says Holy Scripture (Heb. 10:38); that is to say, by means of faith, he sustains himself in the life of grace. When faith grows weak, virtue is in danger; when faith is lost, virtue departs with it. Accordingly, when we are assailed by a temptation to pride or sensuality or any other vice, for self-defense we must instantly arm ourselves with the principles of holy faith. We must direct the eye of our soul to the presence of God or reflect on the sad consequences that follow in the wake of sin, or again on the account we shall have to render on judgment day, and the punishment that awaits the sinner in eternity. Above all we must recall to mind that teaching of holy faith which says that whoever has recourse to God in temptation will be victorious. "I will call upon the Lord," says David, "and I shall be saved from my enemies." (Ps. 17:4).

In fine, faith preserves our peace of heart amid the trials and tribulations that beset us, for in all the crosses of life, faith gives us the assurance that patience and resignation will merit eternal joy. St. Peter the Apostle has said: "If you believe, you shall rejoice with joy unspeakable and glorified, receiving the end of your faith, the salvation of your souls." (1 Peter 1:8–9).

Let us therefore thank God from the bottom of our hearts for having bestowed upon us the inestimable gift of faith. St. Francis de Sales once said: "O God, exceeding great and numerous are the benefits which Thou hast given me! But how shall I ever be able to thank Thee for having bestowed on me the light of holy faith?" And again: "The dignity of our holy faith is so great that I would gladly lay down my life for it." St. Teresa found such consolation in the thought that she belonged to the Holy Catholic Church that at the hour of her death she continued to exclaim: "I am a child of Holy Church, a child of Holy Church." Let us thank God unceasingly for this wonderful grace and be ever mindful of the words of the Psalmist: "He hath not done in like manner to every nation." (Ps. 147:20).

AN OFFERING OF THE INTELLECT

God desires us to use our intellect to know with certainty that it is He who has spoken, not to comprehend all that He asks us to believe.

Reason takes us, as it were, by the hand and leads us into the sanctuary of faith, but itself remains standing at the threshold. Once we are convinced that the truths we are asked to believe really come from God, we are obliged to submit our reason and, on the strength of God's word, to accept as certain the truths proposed, though we may not or cannot understand them. This is that humble simplicity so characteristic of the child, and of which St. Peter speaks when he says: "As newborn babes, desire the rational milk without guile, that thereby you may grow unto salvation." (1 Peter 2:2).

FAITH NOT OPPOSED TO REASON

The mysteries of holy faith are not in opposition to reason, but they transcend its power of comprehension; therefore the futility of trying to fathom them. "Faith," says St. Augustine, "is characteristic not of the proud but of the humble." He who is truly humble never finds it hard to believe. St. Teresa said: "The devil has never succeeded in tempting me against faith. It even seems to me that the less I can comprehend the truths of faith, the more readily I give them my assent."

If you are tempted by the evil spirit against some truth of our holy faith do not stop to consider the difficulties suggested by the devil, but make an act of faith without delay and protest before God your willingness to lay down your very life for the truths of your holy faith. St. Louis, King of France, relates that a learned theologian was once assailed with violent temptations regarding the Real Presence of Jesus Christ in the Blessed Sacrament. He had recourse to the Bishop of Paris, and made known to him his dreadful anxiety; at the same time he begged him with tears to assist him. The Bishop simply asked him if there was anything on earth that could induce him to deny his faith. The theologian protested that nothing could ever cause him to commit so great a crime; whereupon the Bishop quieted him with the assurance that great good would result from the patient endurance of his temptations.

On one occasion when St. Francis de Sales was very ill, he was grievously tormented with doubts in regard to the Blessed Eucharist. Never for a moment did he stop to argue with the devil, but he fought and overcame him with the holy Name of Jesus. When similarly tempted, in all humility, surrender your reason a willing captive; subject yourself to the teachings of Holy Church and strike the tempter with his own weapons, by protesting with zeal and fervor that you are ready to die a thousand times for your holy faith. By acting in this way, you render what Satan intended for your harm an abundant source of merit. Often turn to our Divine Redeemer and address Him in the words of the Apostles: "Lord, increase our faith." (Luke 17:5).

From what we have already seen it is evident that with regard to those truths that surpass our power of comprehension we must subject our reason, and in the words of St. Paul, "bring into captivity our understanding unto the obedience of Christ." (2 Cor. 10:5).

This does not, of course, prevent us from considering the motives that make for the credibility of our holy religion. On the contrary, God wishes us to use our natural powers of intellect to be convinced of the reasonableness of our faith. With this conviction and the assistance of God's grace we shall be more firm in our adherence to all that Holy Church proposes to our belief. As we have said above, the credibility of our holy religion is so clearly established by solid and trust-worthy evidences that any man in his sound senses must needs acknowledge them worthy of credence. We shall briefly consider some of these proofs.

PROOFS OF FAITH

In the first place, the truth of our holy faith is loudly proclaimed by the prophecies of Holy Scripture. These prophecies were uttered hundreds of years ago, and in later years fulfilled to the letter. Thus, for example, the death of our Saviour was foretold by several prophets and the time and circumstances accompanying it minutely described. It was prophesied that the Jews, in punishment for the deicide, would be driven from the temple and the holy land, and hardened and obstinate in sin would be dispersed throughout the world; this prophecy, we know, was literally fulfilled. It was prophesied that after the death of Christ the veneration of heathen deities would give way to the worship of the true God. The event has verified the prediction, for the Apostles of Our Lord, in spite of the innumerable obstacles thrown in their way and armed with no weapons save the cross of Christ, have conquered the world and brought it a captive to faith in the living God.

In the second place, the truth of our holy faith is evident from the miracles which were wrought by our Lord, by His Apostles and the Saints of the Catholic Church as a sanction of her holy teaching. Miracles are beyond the powers of nature. They can happen only by the power of God, to whom all creation is subject. Accordingly, if a religion has real miracles to show in confirmation of her doctrine, that religion must be divine, for it is impossible for God to sanction and promote a false religion by the performance of genuine miracles.

Can the Jews, the heathens, the Mohammedans or the heretics point to a single miracle wrought in favor of their religious tenets? They have no doubt made efforts in the past to deceive the people by trickery and the seemingly miraculous; the deception was soon discovered. But the miracles which God has worked through His servants in every age of the Catholic Church are simply innumerable. In the Catholic Church alone have the words of our Blessed Lord been fulfilled: "Amen, amen I say to you, he that believeth in me, the works that I do he also shall do; and greater than these shall he do." (John 14:12).

Without doubt, in the early days of the Church miracles were more numerous than they are today, since they were necessary for the spread of the Faith. But still they have never been wanting in any age, and they have constantly aided in the conversion of heathen and infidel nations. Numberless miracles were performed, for example, by a St. Francis Xavier, a St. Louis Bertrand, and other holy missionaries in India. Were one to call into question the extraordinary facts recorded in the annals of Church history and in the lives of the Saints, I would simply ask him: By what right do you refuse to believe such men as St. Basil, St. Jerome, St. Gregory and others when you willingly accept what a Tacitus, a Suetonius, or a Pliny has said?

Moreover, God has been pleased to allow certain miracles to go on uninterruptedly in the Church as a continual reproach to the unbelief of the wicked. Recall to mind the famous miracle of the liquefaction of the blood of St. Januarius at Naples. This blood, which usually is found in a hardened, coagulated condition, liquifies several times a year when brought near the head of the Saint. This has been attested by thousands of eyewitnesses. Infidels have tried in vain to find natural explanations for the phenomenon; but the miracle continues to baffle their efforts and to humble their pride.

A third proof for the truth of our holy faith is furnished by the courage and constancy of the martyrs, and this proof is more convincing even than that of miracles. Fifteen Roman emperors in succession used every means in their power to destroy the Christian faith from the face of the earth. Under the reign of Diocletian, who inaugurated the ninth persecution, 17,000 Christians were executed within a single month, not to speak of the thousands who were banished from the country.

According to the account of Genebrard, 11,000,000 martyrs were put to death during the ten great persecutions. If these were gathered within the space of one year, there would be 30,000 martyrs for each day. Now in spite of the fact that these confessors of Christ were subjected to every imaginable torture, such as the tearing of the flesh with iron hooks, roasting their bodies on a gridiron, and burning them with lighted torches, the number of those who were willing and anxious to die for their holy faith was never diminished but seemed always on the increase.

Tiberius, the governor of Palestine, wrote to the Emperor Trajan that there were so many Christians who desired to die as martyrs that it was impossible to execute them all. Hereupon Trajan published an edict in which he commanded the Christians to be left in peace for the future. Now I ask: If the Faith of these valiant martyrs, which is the same that our Holy Church professes today, were not the True Faith of Christ, and had not God assisted them to witness to that Faith with their very blood, would they ever have been able to endure those frightful torments and to deliver themselves up freely and joyfully to a cruel death? Have there been any martyrs in the sects that fell away from the Catholic Church? Have they perhaps a St. Lawrence who offered his roasted limbs to the cruel tyrant for a banquet? Have they perhaps a St. Marcellus or Marcellinus whose feet were pierced with nails; when urged to free themselves from torture by renouncing their holy faith, they replied: "You speak of torments, but we have never experienced a greater joy than at present when we suffer for the love of Jesus Christ." Have they perhaps a St. Processus or a St. Martinian whose bodies were burned with red-hot plates and torn with iron hooks? In the midst of their sufferings they sang hymns of praise to God and yearned to die for Christ.

Add to these martyrs of the first ages the numberless men and women of later days who suffered the most excruciating torments that human cruelty could devise and gave their life for their holy faith. How many died during the 16th century in Japan alone? We select the following facts from the list of cruelties perpetrated during the savage persecution that raged in Japan. A woman named Monica ardently desired to die as a martyr for Christ. To render herself proof against weakness when suffering from the executioners, she practiced beforehand what she thought she might have to endure. One day she grasped a red-hot iron in her hand. Her sister cried out: "O Monica, what are you doing?" "I am preparing myself," she replied, "for a martyr's death. I have already resisted the cravings of hunger and I have overcome that danger. Now I am trying fire so as to be able to endure it when subjected to its torture."

Another woman said to her companions: "I am firmly resolved to give my life for my holy faith. But if at the approach of death you see me tremble, I beg you to drag me by main force to the executioners in order that I may share your crown." A boy named Anthony replied to his parents, who begged him with tears to renounce his faith: "Cease torturing me with your words and complaints; I am resolved once and for all to die for the love of Jesus Christ." And when, like his Divine Master, he hung on the cross, he intoned the words of the 112th Psalm: "Praise the Lord, ye children." He sang it as far as the "Glory be to the Father," when he expired and went to complete the hymn of praise in Heaven. Another boy said to his father: "I will rather suffer death at the hands of the executioners or at your own hands than refuse obedience to God; I will not cast myself into Hell for the sake of pleasing any man." A servant spoke thus to his master: "I know what Heaven is worth; and since a martyr's death is the shortest road that leads me thither I choose it with joy, and I esteem my earthly life as little as the dust beneath my feet."

A woman by the name of Ursula had seen her husband and her two children put to death for their faith; with tears in her eyes she exclaimed: "I thank Thee, my God, that Thou hast deemed me worthy to make this offering; grant me also the crown which now adorns my loved ones. All I have left is the little child I carry in my arms. I gladly offer it with myself; graciously accept this last offering which I make to Thee." She then pressed the child to her heart, and one stroke of the sword beheaded the mother and the daughter.

Another mother called out continually to her son who, like herself, was fastened to a cross: "Courage, my son, courage! We are on the way to Heaven. Continue to call on Jesus and Mary." A nobleman named Simon said: "What a happiness for me to be permitted to die for my Redeemer! How have I ever deserved so great a favor?" A little blind girl of eight years clung closely to her mother so as to be able to die with her on the funeral pyre. A boy of five years of age was roused out of sleep to be led off to a cruel death. Without betraying the least alarm he put on his best clothes and was then carried off to the place of execution. On their arrival the little lad himself offered his neck to the executioner.

The latter was so moved at the sight of this tender child that he was unable to perform his duty. Another had to take his place, and it was only after several strokes of the sword that an end was put to the child's life. All these facts were attested by declared enemies of our Holy Church.

Once more the proof of our holy faith becomes evident when we consider that from the time of the Apostles down to our own days our Faith has continued unaltered. The Apostles and their successors were careful to preserve the doctrine of our Divine Redeemer in its primitive purity and integrity. Christ Himself imposed upon them this sacred duty when He said: "Going therefore, teach ye all nations; teach them to observe all things whatsoever I have commanded you." (Matt. 28:19–20). Therefore St. John exhorts the faithful: "Let that which you have heard from the beginning abide in you." (1 John 2:24).

The Apostle Jude writes: "I beseech you, dearly beloved, to contend earnestly for the faith once delivered to the saints." (Jude 3).

Similar are the exhortations of the Apostle St. Paul when writing to the Ephesians: "I beseech you, brethren, that you be careful to keep the unity of the Spirit in the bond of peace" (Eph. 4:3), and to the Corinthians:

"Let there be no schisms among you; but be perfect in the same mind and in the same judgment." (1 Cor. 1:10).

These admonitions of the Apostle have always been strictly adhered to by the pastors of the Church, for, in the words of St. Augustine, "What they found in the Church they have preserved, and what their fathers handed down to them they in turn left as a precious legacy to their sons." Accordingly, the Catholic Church has remained the same in all ages and in all climes. The doctrines she teaches today are the same that were taught and believed in the first ages of the Church. The sects, on the contrary, that have separated from the Catholic Church, have not remained unchanged in the doctrines which they propound. If you desire an illustration of this, read the History of the Variations by the famous Bishop Bossuet. There you will find an authentic record of the everchanging tenets of the Protestant denominations. The pride that caused the founders of these sects to refuse obedience to the true Church of Christ has led their followers in turn to refuse obedience to them, and thus countless new doctrines and new religions have sprung into existence. It is of immense advantage for us who are faithful adherents of the true Church of God to read and ponder the accounts that are found in the history of heresies. Such a reflection is calculated to bring into a most favorable light our own True Faith that, like our Saviour Himself, is "yesterday, and today, and the same forever." (Heb. 13:8). It will foster in us a spirit of loyal submission to our Holy Church, and a deep sense of gratitude to God for the inestimable gift of the True Faith.

A LIVING FAITH

To be pleasing and acceptable in the sight of God, it is not enough merely to believe all that our holy faith teaches us; we must, moreover, regulate our life in accordance with our belief. Pico of Mirandola says: "It is certainly great folly not to wish to believe the Gospel of Christ; but it would be greater folly still to believe it and to live as if you did not believe it." The unbelieving act very irrationally when they close their eyes so as not to see the abyss towards which they are hastening. But what of the folly of those among the faithful who see the abyss, and with open eyes actually hurl themselves into it? "O my brethren," exclaims St. James, "what shall it profit if a man say he hath faith, but hath not works? Shall faith be able to save him?" (James 2:14).

Many Christians believe without doubt that there is a just God who will judge them; that endless happiness or eternal misery awaits them; and yet they live as though there were no God, no judgment, no Heaven and no Hell. There are many who believe that our Divine Redeemer was born in the stable at Bethlehem, lived for 30 years in the humble abode at Nazareth, supported Himself by the labor of His hands, and at last, consumed with suffering and sorrow, ended His life on an infamous gibbet; and yet they do not love Him; indeed, they offend Him by innumerable sins. It is to these that St. Bernard addresses his words of warning: "Show by your deeds that you believe; by a virtuous life a Christian must prove that he has faith."

The sinful man who knows the truths of faith, and does not live in accordance with them, has a very weak faith, to say the least. For it stands to reason that if a man firmly believed that the grace of God is the highest and best good he could possess, and that sin robs us of grace and is the greatest evil in this world, he must of necessity change his life. When, therefore, the sinner prefers the miserable goods of this world to his Lord and God, he gives evident proof that he has a very weak faith, if any at all. St. Bernard says: "He who acknowledges God with his tongue but denies Him in deed, dedicates his tongue to the Lord and his soul to the devil." According to the Apostle St. James, that faith which does not manifest itself by works, is dead. (James 2:17).

If we see a man who betrays no sign of life, and who neither moves, nor speaks, nor breathes, we say he is no longer alive but dead. In like manner, that faith which gives no evidence of vitality by the performance of works of eternal life, we rightly regard as dead. There are Christians who willingly accept those teachings of our holy faith that are confined to the sphere of the intellect, but who give no proof whatever that they believe the truths which affect the will. And yet the latter are as certain and undoubted as the former, for they are all made known to us by one and the same Gospel of Christ. If we believe the doctrine of the Blessed Trinity and the Incarnation of the Divine Word, we must also accept the principles that Christ our Lord has laid down for the regulation of our conduct. It was with this end in view that St. Paul wrote thus to his disciples: "Try your own selves if you be in the faith; prove ye yourselves." (2 Cor. 13:5). Our Blessed Redeemer has said: "Blessed are the poor in spirit: for theirs is the kingdom of heaven." (Matt 5:3).

Now if a man complains of the dispositions of Divine Providence because he happens to be poor, such a man cannot be called truly faithful, for the man who believes from his heart the words of our Blessed Lord, will seek his riches and his happiness not in the perishable goods of this earth but in the grace of God and eternal life. When gold and silver and precious stones were offered to St. Clement on condition that he would renounce Christ, the Saint heaved a deep sigh and complained bitterly that with such a miserable and contemptible exchange they should try to rob him of his God. Our Divine Redeemer has said: "Blessed are the peacemakers! Blessed are they that mourn! Blessed are they that suffer persecution for justice' sake!" (Matt. 5:9). By this He meant to say: Blessed are they that suffer sickness, and temporal loss or some other misfortune with patience and resignation. Blessed are they that suffer persecution because they flee from sin or endeavor to promote the glory of God! He who thinks that he disgraces himself when he forgives; he whose only concern is to live an easy and agreeable life and to shun the very shadow of self-denial; he who pities those who renounce the joys and pleasures of earth and crucify their flesh; he who from human respect neglects the practices of piety and the reception of the

Sacraments and is wholly absorbed with the attractions of the theater and ballroom can have no valid claim to the title of a faithful Catholic.

This seems to be the place to correct a false impression that is very prevalent. There are many who imagine that a life in harmony with the precepts of our holy faith must necessarily be a sad and joyless life. The devil pictures our holy religion to them as a tyrant who imposes only burdens and cares upon her children, forces them to constant self-renunciation and interdicts the gratification of every desire. There is no doubt that for those whose only desire is to satisfy their sensual cravings, a life in accordance with holy faith has little that is attractive. "They that are Christ's," says the Apostle, "have crucified their flesh with the vices and concupiscences." (Gal. 5:24).

The law of Jesus Christ commands us to battle against our inordinate inclinations, to love our enemies, to mortify our body, to be patient in adversities and to place all our hope in the life to come. But all this does not make the life of the truly faithful a sad and sorrowful one. The religion of Jesus Christ says to us, as it were: Come and unite yourselves to Me; I will lead you along a path which to the bodily eyes seems rough and hard to climb, but to those of good will is easy and agreeable. You seek peace and pleasure? Well and good! Which peace is to be preferred? That which, when scarcely tasted, disappears and leaves the heart replete with bitterness, or that which will rejoice and satiate you for all eternity? You strive for honors? Very well! Which do you prefer, that empty honor that disappears like a puff of smoke, or that true and genuine honor which will one day glorify you before the whole world? Ask those who lead a life of faith if the renunciation of this world's goods makes them sad! Visit the holy Anchorite Paul in his grotto, St. Francis of Assisi on Mount Alverno, St. Mary Magdalen de Pazzi in her convent and ask them if they miss the joys and pleasures of this earth! They will answer without hesitation: No, no; we desire but God alone and nothing else.

Should anyone object that a life according to faith is opposed to nature, I answer: It is, no doubt, opposed to nature—but to a depraved and fallen nature. It is burdensome, yes, but only for those who rely on their own strength and resources. But for one who trusts in God and begs for His assistance, the observance of the law of Jesus Christ is sweet and easy. "Taste and see," says the Psalmist, "how sweet is the Lord." (Ps. 33:9). "Come to me, all you that labor and are burdened, and I will refresh you. Take up my yoke upon you and learn of me because I am meek and humble of heart: and you shall find rest to your souls. For my yoke is sweet and my burden light." (Matt. 11:28–30).

Chapter II

Hope

"In thee, O Lord, have I hoped, let me never be confounded."—Psalms 30:2

Hope is a supernatural virtue by which we confidently expect, in virtue of God's promise, the endless happiness of Heaven and the means necessary for its attainment. To be convinced of the inestimable value of this virtue, and to have a constant incentive for its practice, it will be profitable to consider the objects of our hope, its motives, its qualities, and its effects.

The first and foremost object of our hope, the object by excellence, is the possession of God in Heaven. We are not to suppose that the hope of possessing God in Heaven in any way interferes with the virtue of love. They are not opposed; in fact, the hope of eternal happiness is inseparably united with love, for only in Heaven will the completion and perfection of love be found. According to St. Thomas, with the idea of friendship is intimately united the mutual sharing of goods, for as friendship is nothing else but a mutual attraction it follows that friends must do as much good to one another as is in their power. Without this mutual sharing of goods, says the Angelic Doctor, there can be no genuine friendship. (Ia IIae, Q. 65, a. 5). Our Lord called His disciples His friends because He communicated His mysteries to them: "I have called you friends because all things whatsoever I have heard of my Father, I have made known to you." (John 15:15). According to the teaching of St. Thomas, love does not exclude the hope of the reward which God has prepared for us in Heaven; that very reward is the principal object of our love, for it is nothing but God Himself, the vision of whom is the eternal happiness of the elect. "Friendship," says the Angelic Doctor, "requires that a friend be in possession of his friend." This is that mutual communication or surrender of which the spouse in the Canticle speaks when she says: "My beloved is mine and I am his." (Cant. 2:16). In Heaven the soul gives itself entirely to God and God gives Himself entirely to the soul, as far as its capacity and merits will allow.

Love, says Dionysius the Areopagite, strives, in accordance with its nature, after union with the object loved; or rather, as St. Augustine remarks, love is a golden chain which binds together the hearts of the lover and the loved one. But since this union cannot be effected between those that are separated, the lover continually yearns for the presence of his beloved. When the spouse in the Canticle saw herself separated from her Beloved she was consumed with longing and begged her companions to make known to Him her anguish, to induce Him to afford her some consolation by His presence: "I adjure you, O daughters of Jerusalem, if you find my beloved, that you tell him that I languish with love." (Cant. 5:8). A soul that tenderly loves Jesus Christ cannot live here below without the most ardent longing to be united with Him in Heaven, where He will be her reward exceeding great.

As long, therefore, as our soul is not perfectly united with God in Heaven, it will never enjoy true peace. Those who love Our Lord sincerely find peace of heart, it is true, in conformity to the will of God; but perfect peace and perfect rest they shall never have here below. This we shall acquire only with the attainment of our last end, the vision of God face to face and His ineffable love. As long as the soul is separated from her last end she shall continue to sigh with the prophet: "Behold in peace is my bitterness most bitter." (Is. 38:17). Yes, my God, I live in peace in this valley of tears, for such is Thy holy will; but I cannot but remember, with unspeakable pain, that I am not as yet perfectly united with Thee, the Source of all peace and rest, the Goal of my heart's desire. It was for this reason that the Saints yearned for their heavenly home, consumed as they were with an ardent love for God. Holy David complained about his long and weary exile: "Woe is me that my sojourning is prolonged." (Ps. 119:5). Only the hope of eternal happiness could console him: "I shall be satisfied when thy glory shall appear." (Ps. 16:15). St. Paul desired nothing more ardently than to leave this world and to be with Christ: "I desire to be dissolved and to be with Christ." (Phil. 1:23).

"The good that I hope for," says St. Francis of Assisi, "is so great that every suffering becomes for me a pleasure." All these expressions of ardent longing are so many acts of perfect love. St. Thomas teaches that the highest degree of love that a soul on earth can attain is an ardent desire for Heaven, to be there united to God and to possess Him forever. The greatest suffering that the souls in Purgatory endure proceeds from this longing for the possession of God, and this pain is felt especially by those who in life had but a feeble desire for Heaven. Cardinal Bellarmine thinks that in Purgatory there is a place where souls endure no pains of sense, but are tortured solely by the loss of the presence of God. (De Purg., 1. 2, c. 7). St. Gregory, St. Vincent Ferrer, St. Bridget and St. Bede the Venerable cite a number of such instances where souls are tormented not on account of sins committed, but because of the absence of a desire for Heaven. There are souls that strive after perfection, but without any special desire to leave this earth and to be united to God. But since eternal life is a priceless treasure that Jesus Christ has purchased for us by His death, those souls that have but a feeble desire to possess it will have to suffer later on this account. There are three things necessary for the attainment of eternal life: the pardon of our sins, the victory over temptations, and the crown of all graces, a holy death. These three things are accordingly the objects of our hope.

THE PARDON OF OUR SINS

"Thou hast sinned, O Christian," says St. John Chrysostom, "but dost thou desire forgiveness? Fear not, for God's desire to grant it is greater than your desire to receive it." If God sees an unfortunate wretch in sin, He waits for a favorable opportunity to show him mercy. At times He reveals to him the punishment he has deserved, to urge him to enter into himself. "Thou hast given a warning to them that fear thee: that they may flee from before the bow." (Ps. 59:6). At times He knocks on the door of the sinner's heart, hoping that He may open it: "Behold I stand before the gate and knock." (Apoc. 3:20). Sometimes He goes after the sinner and calls to him like a compassionate father: Why will you be lost? "Why will you die, O house of Israel?" (Ezech. 18:31). Dionysius says that God even begs us not to hurl ourselves into perdition. This is confirmed by the Apostle when he beseeches the sinner in the name of Jesus Christ to be reconciled with his God: "For Christ, we beseech you, be reconciled to God." (2 Cor. 5:20). St. Chrysostom remarks: Christ Himself requests you, and what is His request? "Be reconciled to God." (2 Cor.). If, in spite of all this, there are hard and obstinate hearts that refuse to yield, what more is there that the Lord can do for them? Yet even such has He promised not to repel if they return truly repentant: "Him that cometh to me I will not cast out." (John 6:37). He declares that He is ready and willing to receive everyone who comes to Him: "Turn ye to me, saith the Lord of hosts, and I will turn to you." (Zach. 1:3).

To every sinner who desires to repent, He promises pardon: "But if the wicked do penance for all his sins which he hath committed, and keep all my commandments and do judgment and justice, living he shall live, and shall not die. I will not remember all his iniquities that he hath done." (Ezech. 18:21–22). Yes, He even goes so far as to say: "Come and accuse me: if your sins be as scarlet, they shall be made as white as snow: and if they be red as crimson, they shall be white as wool." (Is. 1:18). The royal Psalmist says: "A contrite and humbled heart, O God, thou wilt not despise." (Ps. 50:19). In the Gospel of St. Luke we have a beautiful picture of the joy with which the shepherd receives the lost sheep, and the love that the father manifests on the return of the prodigal son. And these are God's own words: "I say to you that even so there shall be joy in heaven upon one sinner that doth penance, more than upon ninety-nine just who need not penance." (Luke 15:7). The reason for this, according to St. Gregory, is that the repentant sinner generally loves God more ardently than the just man, who is apt to grow lukewarm in His service.

It is doubtless true that we shall have a strict account to render of all the sins we have committed, but who will be our judge? St. John tells us: "Neither doth the Father judge any man, but hath given all judgment to the Son." (John 5:22). It is to our Redeemer, then, that the judgment has been entrusted, and St. Paul encourages us with the words: "Who is he that shall condemn? Christ Jesus that died, yea that is risen also again, who also maketh intercession for us." (Rom. 8:34). We shall be judged by a loving Redeemer who, to save us from eternal death, delivered Himself to death, and not content with that, now acts as our advocate with the Father in Heaven. "Why should you fear, O sinner," says St. Thomas of Villanova, "as long as you detest your sins? How could He condemn who died that He might not have to condemn? How could He reject the repentant sinner, since He came down from Heaven to seek that sinner?"

St. Chrysostom says that every single wound of Jesus Christ is a mouth that eloquently pleads with God for the forgiveness of our sins. In the revelations of St. Mary Magdalen de Pazzi we read that one day God spoke to her in the following words: "Through the revenge I took on the body of My Son, My justice has been changed into clemency. His blood cries not for vengeance, as did the blood of Abel; it asks for mercy, and My justice cannot resist its pleading. The blood of Jesus binds the hands of Justice so that they cannot be raised, as once they were, to punish." The holy Fathers teach that he who detests the evil he has committed, can be certain of the forgiveness of his sins. Now, according to the words of St. Teresa, everyone who is ready to die rather than offend God anew can say that he truly hates his sins. If you, therefore, dear Christian, entertain sentiments such as these, why are you tortured with fear and distrust? Reanimate your courage at the sight of so many saints who lived for a long time at enmity with God, but returned to Him repentant and sorry, conscious that they dreaded a new offense against God more than death itself, and full of hope for the pardon of their sins.

St. Afra of Ratisbon was formerly a heathen and so immoral that her very home was a house of assignation. Afterward, with her mother and her whole family, she was converted to Christianity. From Ruinart's Acts of the Martyrs we learn that the abomination of her sins was continually before her eyes and caused her intense grief. On becoming Christian, she distributed her ill-gotten gains to the poor. If there happened to be any who refused to accept what she had acquired by her offenses against God, she begged them with tears to recommend her to God that she might be pardoned her sins. Just at this time the persecution of Diocletian was raging. The saint was taken captive and brought before a judge named Cajus. "Sacrifice to the gods," he said to her; "that will be better for you than to be tortured to death." The saint replied: "To my grief, I sinned before I knew the true God; therefore it is impossible for me to do what you require. To sacrifice to the gods would be a fresh offense against my Divine Master, and that I will never commit." The judge ordered her to be led to the temple to sacrifice; she replied with great firmness: "My temple is Jesus Christ who is always present to me and before whom I daily confess my sins. As I am unable to offer Him any other sacrifice, I yearn to offer Him the sacrifice of myself, that this body which has offended Him may be purified by the sufferings which I shall gladly bear."

"But what can you expect from the God of the Christians," said Cajus, "after the shameful life you have led? You had better sacrifice to our gods." The saint replied: "My Saviour Jesus Christ declared that He came down from Heaven to save the sinner. In the Gospel we read that a sinful woman washed the feet of Jesus with her tears and obtained the pardon of all her sins. Moreover, the Saviour never spurned the sinner unmercifully, but we are told He received sinners and even ate with them."

When he found that his efforts proved unavailing, Cajus said: "If you refuse to sacrifice I will have you tortured and burned alive." The saint courageously replied: "Gladly will I submit my body to any torment, for it has been the instrument of many sins, but I will never defile my soul by sacrificing to the devil." Thereupon the judge pronounced the sentence of death. Afra raised her eyes to Heaven and uttered the following prayer: "My Lord Jesus Christ, Thou who hast come to call not the just but sinners to repentance and hast given the sinner the assurance of pardon when he returns repentant to Thee, receive me, a poor sinner; I gladly submit to this torture for love of Thee; grant that this fire which consumes my body, may preserve my soul from Hell." When the flames had mounted and closed above her head she was still heard to say: "I thank Thee, my Lord, that Thou who wast Innocence itself didst offer Thyself for poor sinners. O Blessed of the Father, who didst die for our wretched and sin-stained souls, I thank Thee once more and I offer myself to Thee who livest and reignest with the Father and the Holy Spirit forever and ever. Amen." As she ended her prayer, her soul took its flight to God.

VICTORY OVER TEMPTATION

Besides the pardon of our sins, we must confidently hope for the victory over our temptations. In order to persevere in well-doing, our confidence must not rest on our good resolutions. When we build on the foundation of our own strength our edifice is sure to fall. To maintain ourselves in the grace of God it is necessary, therefore, to place our hope in the merits of Jesus Christ. With His assistance we shall persevere till death, even though we be assailed by all the powers of earth and Hell. There may be times when temptations are so violent that sin seems unavoidable. We must be on our guard at such times not to lose courage and give up the struggle. Our only resource is to hasten to Jesus Crucified. He and He alone can sustain us. The Lord permits that from time to time even the Saints have such storms to endure. St. Paul says of himself: "We were pressed out of measure above our strength, so that we were weary even of life." (2 Cor. 1:8).

The Apostle here shows what he was when left to his own strength; and he wishes, doubtless, to teach us how God permits us at times to experience our own weakness in order that we may acknowledge our misery and "trust not in ourselves, but in God who raiseth the dead" (2 Cor. 1:9), humbly asking His help that we may not succumb. In another place the Apostle teaches the same truth more distinctly still: "In all things we suffer tribulation, but are not distressed; we are straitened, but are not destitute . . . we are cast down, but we perish not." (2 Cor. 4:8–9). We are bowed down by sorrow and harassed by passion, but yet we do not despair. We are tossed about on a stormy sea, but we do not suffer shipwreck, because the Lord by His grace gives us strength to resist our enemies.

At the same time the Apostle bids us not to forget that we are weak and frail creatures who may easily lose the treasure of divine grace, and we can preserve it only by the power of God: "We have this treasure in earthen vessels, that the excellency may be of the power of God, and not of us." (2 Cor. 4:7).

Although, as we have already seen, the power to avoid sin is not from ourselves but from the grace of God, we must at the same time be careful not to render ourselves weaker than we already are. There are certain faults that we consider of no account, and yet they may be the reason why God withdraws His supernatural light, and thus the power of the devil is increased. Such faults are the desire to be regarded as learned and distinguished by the world; vanity in dress; the seeking for superfluous comforts and luxuries; the habit of showing oneself offended by every unkind word or want of attention; the inordinate desire to please others; the omission of exercises of piety from human respect; disobedience in little things; little aversions that are fostered in the heart; little lies and jokes at the expense of charity; loss of time through idle conversations or a greediness for news; in a word, every attachment for earthly things, and every gratification of self-love may give the enemy an opportunity of accomplishing our destruction. At all events, faults of this kind committed with deliberation deprive us of that assistance of Our Lord which would protect us from falling into sin.

A HAPPY DEATH

We hope, in fine, for the grace of a happy death. The hour of death is for us the time of greatest anxiety. Jesus Christ alone can give us the strength to suffer, with patience and profit, the trials of this last decisive moment. At the approach of death we have more than ever to fear from the assaults of Hell. The nearer we approach our goal, the more will Hell strive to prevent our reaching it. St. Eleazar, who had lived a life of great purity, was violently tempted in the hour of death, but he did not lose courage for a moment. To those standing around him he said: "The efforts of Hell at this moment are very great, but by the merits of His suffering our Saviour takes from them all their power." St. Francis desired that at the hour of his death the Passion of Christ be read to him, and St. Charles Borromeo had pictures representing the suffering Saviour placed on his bed; while gazing at these he gave up his soul to God. Our Lord Jesus wished to suffer death, as St. Paul says, "that through death he might destroy him who had the empire of death, that is to say, the devil; and might deliver them, who through the fear of death were all their lifetime subject to servitude." (Heb. 2:14–15).

Therefore, says the same Apostle, "It behooved him in all things to be made like unto his brethren, that he might become merciful." (Heb. 2:17). The Lord wished to assume human nature and its miseries, sin and ignorance and concupiscence excepted, and why? In order that He might Himself experience our misery, the better to have compassion on us, for misery is better learned by suffering it than by seeing it in others. In this way Our Lord became more inclined to assist us in all the temptations of life, and especially at the hour of death. Should the devil therefore assail us in life or at death, bringing before us the sins of our youth, we must say to him with St. Bernard: "What I need to enter Heaven, I appropriate from the merits of Jesus Christ who suffered and died in order to procure for me that glory of which I was unworthy." (In Cant. 61).

MOTIVES FOR OUR HOPE

As to the motives on which our hope should rest, the first we find in the promises made by God. On nearly every page of Holy Scripture we find reasons for hoping in the Lord. We read there that God promises eternal salvation and the means to attain it to those who believe and pray: "All things, whatsoever you ask when ye pray, believe that you shall receive; and they shall come unto you." (Mark 11:24). "Every one that asketh receiveth." (Matt. 7:8). "The Lord is the protection of all that trust in him." (Ps. 17:31). "My children behold the generations of men; and know ye that no one hath hoped in the Lord and hath been confounded." (Ecclus. 2:11). "None of them that wait on thee shall be confounded." (Ps. 24:3). "In thee, O Lord, have I hoped; I shall not be confounded forever." (Ps. 70:1).

"Because he trusteth in me I will deliver him, and I will glorify him." (Ps. 90:14–15). "Amen, amen, I say to you: if you ask the Father any thing in my name, he will give it to you." (John 16:23).

These and countless other promises are made to all men without exception. Heaven and earth shall pass away, as Scripture says, but the words and promises of God shall not pass away. "Let us therefore," in the words of the Apostle, "hold fast the confession of our hope without wavering, for he is faithful that hath promised." (Heb. 10:23).

The second motive of our hope is the sincere desire of Our Lord to make us happy. God loves all His creatures. "Thou lovest all things that are, and hatest none of the things which thou hast made." (Wis. 11:25). But every love, says St. Augustine, possesses an active force and cannot remain idle. Consequently, love contains in its very essence the idea of benevolence, and one who loves cannot but do good to the object of his love if it is at all possible for him. "Love," says Aristotle, "endeavors to accomplish what it considers good for the object loved." If, therefore, God loves all men, He must also desire that all men attain eternal happiness, for this is the highest and only good of man since it is the end for which man was created. "You have your fruit unto sanctification, and the end life everlasting." (Rom. 6:22).

Calvin was guilty of a horrible blasphemy when he said that God had created some men only to cast them into Hell. He even dared to assert that God forces men to sin in order that they may be damned. "God will have all men to be saved and to come to the knowledge of the truth." (1 Tim. 2:4). He declares that He wishes for the conversion and salvation even of the ungodly who have deserved eternal death. "As I live, saith the Lord God, I desire not the death of the wicked, but that the wicked turn from his way and live." (Ezech. 33:11). Tertullian calls attention to the fact that in using the words: "As I live," the Lord pronounces an oath in order that we might believe Him without hesitation. It is therefore a matter of great surprise to the learned Petavius that anyone could call this truth into question. "If an attempt is made," says he, "to misconstrue so clear a text of Sacred Scripture which God even confirms with an oath, what is there left in matters of faith that is safe from the falsifiers?" But why does God so ardently desire the salvation of all men? Simply because He has created them from love and He has loved them from all eternity.

"Yea I have loved thee with an everlasting love, therefore have I drawn thee, taking pity on thee." (Jer. 31:3). We read in the Epistle of St. Peter that the Lord, knowing the weakness of man, has patience with the sinner and does not wish him to be lost, but to do penance and be saved. "The Lord dealeth patiently for your sake, not willing that any should perish but that all should return to penance." (2 Peter 3:9). In short, God desires to save all men and if there are some unhappy creatures who force Him, by their sins, to condemn them, He speaks to them, as it were, in tears of compassion, and says: "Why will you die, O house of Israel? Convert and live." (Ezech. 18:31–32). Why will you be lost, my children, and condemn yourselves to eternal perdition? If you have been so unhappy as to leave Me, return to Me now repentant and I will restore to you the life you have lost.

Judge for yourself then, Christian soul, if it be not true that God desires your eternal salvation. For the future, therefore, never give expression to such sentiments as: Who knows; perhaps God does not wish me to be saved! Perhaps on account of my offenses He desires me to be lost forever! Such thoughts you must banish from your mind, as it must now be evident to you that God assists you with His grace and urgently invites you to His love.

As a third and powerful motive for hope in God, we have the merits of Jesus Christ. Long before our Saviour had appeared on earth, the royal Psalmist David placed all his hope in Him: "Into thy hands I commend my spirit: thou hast redeemed me, O Lord, the God of truth." (Ps. 30:6). How much more, therefore, ought we to place our confidence in Jesus now that He has come and accomplished the work of our redemption. Full of trust and assurance, we ought to repeat with the royal Psalmist: "Into Thy hands O Lord, I commend my spirit: Thou hast redeemed me, O Lord, the God of truth." Thou art faithful to Thy promises.

If on account of our sins we have good reason to fear eternal death, we have still stronger motives for hope of eternal life in the merits of Jesus Christ, which are incomparably more powerful to save than our sins are to destroy us. By our sins we have deserved eternal death, but our Redeemer has come to our assistance, says the prophet Isaias, and taken upon Himself our debts in order to make satisfaction for them by His sufferings: "He hath borne our infirmities and carried our sorrows." (Is. 53:4). At that unhappy moment when we committed sin, God wrote the sentence of our eternal doom. But what has Jesus Christ accomplished? He has taken this sentence of condemnation, as the Apostle says, fastened it to the Cross and blotted it out with His Precious Blood. We can never look upon that sentence without seeing the Cross on which it was destroyed, and thus our hope of forgiveness and of eternal salvation is revived: "Blotting out the handwriting of the decree that was against us. . . . And he hath taken the same out of the way, fastening it to the cross." (Col. 2:14). "Let us go therefore with confidence to the throne of grace; that we may obtain mercy, and find grace in seasonable aid." (Heb. 4:16).

The throne of grace is the Cross on which Our Lord was exalted in order to dispense mercy and grace to all who have recourse to Him. But we must go to Him at once, while we have an opportunity of finding assistance; otherwise, we may come too late, and seek in vain. Let us hasten, therefore, to the Cross of Christ and embrace it with unwavering confidence. We need not be frightened at the sight of our misery; in Christ we shall find riches and treasures of grace: "I give thanks to my God," says the Apostle, "that in all things you are made rich in him. . . . so that nothing is wanting to you in any grace." (1 Cor. 1:4, 5, 7). The merits of Jesus Christ have opened to us the treasury of

God by acquiring for us a right to all the graces that we can possibly desire.

St. Leo says that the advantages which accrue to us through the death of Jesus Christ are far greater than the losses the devil has occasioned us by sin. St. Paul tells us the same: "Not as the offense, so also the gift . . . for where sin abounded, grace did more abound." (Rom. 5:15, 20).

Therefore, our Saviour exhorts us to hope for all graces through His infinite merits. He Himself teaches us how to present our petitions to His heavenly Father: "Amen, amen I say to you: if you ask the Father any thing in my name, he will give it you." (John 16:23). "He that spared not even his own Son, but delivered him up for us all, how hath he not also, with him, given us all things?" (Rom. 8:32). According to the Apostles, therefore, God has excepted nothing, neither the forgiveness of sins, nor final perseverance, nor divine love and perfection, nor Heaven itself; "with him he hath given us all things." The only thing for us to do is to ask Him for His graces, for "the Lord is rich unto all that call upon him." (Rom. 10:12).

CHRIST'S INTERCESSION

Do not forget, says the Venerable John of Avila, that between the Eternal Father and ourselves there is a Mediator, Jesus Christ, to whom we are united by bonds of love so strong that nothing can ever break them unless we ourselves break them by mortal sin. The blood of Jesus Christ cries for mercy in our behalf, and that cry is so loud that the clamor of our sins cannot be heard. No one is lost, therefore, because satisfaction has not been made for him, but because by the neglect of the Sacraments he fails to share in the satisfaction which Jesus Christ has made. Christ Our Lord has taken it upon Himself to remedy our ills as if they were His own. He who was without sin, took upon Himself our sins and prayed for forgiveness for them. And He prayed to His heavenly Father with as much fervor as if He were praying for Himself. What He desired, He obtained. God willed that we should be so inseparably united to Jesus Christ that He cannot be loved except we be loved with Him; nor can we be hated except He be hated with us. But now Jesus cannot be hated; therefore, we shall be loved as long as we remain united to Him by love.

Jesus is loved by His heavenly Father; therefore we are loved with Him. He is far more powerful to win God's love for us than we are to draw His hatred on ourselves, for God loves His Divine Son more than He hates the sinner. Our Lord spoke thus to His heavenly Father: "Father, I will that where I am, they also whom thou hast given me, may be with me." (John 17:24). As love is stronger than hatred, love carries off the victory. Our sins are forgiven and the love of God bestowed on us and the strength of the bond of love gives us the assurance that God will never forsake us. "Can a woman forget her infant . . . ?" says the prophet Isaias; "and if she should forget, yet will not I forget thee. Behold, I have graven thee in my hands." (Is. 49:15–16).

The Lord has written us in His hands with His own blood. Therefore we should allow nothing to disquiet us, for He arranges and disposes everything with these very hands which were nailed to the Cross as a proof of His love for us.

THE INTERCESSION OF THE BLESSED MOTHER

A fourth motive for unbounded confidence is the powerful intercession of Mary our Mother. St. Bernard says that we have access to the Eternal Father through His Divine Son, who is a mediator of justice. But we have access to the Son through His holy Mother, who is the mediatrix of grace and who, by her intercession, has obtained for us what Jesus Christ has merited by His death. "Through thee who hast found grace, may we have access to the Son, O Mother of our Salvation, in order that through thee He may receive us who through thee was given to us." All goods and graces, therefore, that we receive from God come to us through the intercession of Mary. And why is this? St. Bernard replies: "Because God has wished it so."

A further reason of this privilege of Mary, St. Augustine gives us when he says: "Mary can rightly be called our Mother because by her love she contributed towards giving us the life of grace and making us members of the mystic body of Christ." As Mary, therefore, by her love contributed towards the spiritual regeneration of the faithful, God has willed that through her intercession all men shall obtain the life of grace here and the life of glory hereafter. On this account the Church desires us to invoke her as "our life, our sweetness and our hope." Accordingly, St. Bernard exhorts us to have constant recourse to this divine Mother because her petitions are certainly answered. "Hasten to Mary," he writes, "for I say it without hesitation, the Son will certainly hear the Mother. She is the ladder of safety for poor sinners. She is my greatest assurance; she is the only ground of my hope." He calls Mary a ladder for sinners, for as you cannot mount to the third round before putting the foot on the second, nor to the second before reaching the first, so you can reach God only through Jesus Christ, and Jesus Christ only through Mary. The Saint calls Mary his greatest assurance and the only ground of his hope, for it is his firm conviction that God desires all graces that He bestows on us to come through the hands of Mary.

Be of good heart then, ye children of Mary! You know that she regards as her children all who desire to be so. Courage, therefore, and confidence! How can you fear that you will ever perish when such a Mother defends and protects you? He who loves this good Mother and places himself under her protection can say with St. Bonaventure: "I rejoice and am glad, for my sentence on judgment day depends on Jesus my

Brother and on Mary my Mother." This very thought filled St. Anselm with consolation and joy: "O blessed confidence! O safe refuge!" he cried, "The Mother of God is also my Mother; with what security I can hope for eternal happiness, for that happiness depends on the decision of a good Brother and on a compassionate Mother."

QUALITIES OF HOPE

We shall now devote our attention to the qualities that should characterize our hope. First of all, our hope must be firm and unwavering. "Hope of eternal happiness," according to St. Thomas, "is the confident expectation of this happiness." With this doctrine the Council of Trent agrees when it says: "We must all confidently hope for the assistance of God; for as God has begun the good work in us, He wills to complete it, provided we make use of His grace; both the desire and its realization are from Him." (Sess. 6, ch. 18). This is what the Apostle St. Paul taught in his letter to Timothy: "I know whom I have believed, and I am certain that he is able to keep that which I have committed unto him, against that day." (2 Tim. 1:12). In this we see the distinction between Christian hope and that which is purely human. With human hope there is always connected the fear that the person who has made a promise has changed or will change his mind. Christian hope, on the contrary, which looks to eternal salvation, has no doubt or fear whatever regarding God. The Lord is able and willing to grant us eternal happiness, and what is more He has promised it to all who keep His commandments; for this end He pledges Himself to grant to all who seek them the graces necessary to fulfill His commands. It is nevertheless true that even Christian hope is not altogether free from a certain fear; but as St. Thomas says: "We have nothing to fear on the part of God, but only from ourselves." It is quite possible that we may fail to cooperate with God's grace and even place obstacles in its way.

The Council of Trent was right, therefore, in condemning the innovators for saying that man has no freedom of will, and that each one must have an infallible certainty with regard to his perseverance in grace and eternal happiness. This doctrine the Council condemned because, as we have just seen, our cooperation is necessary for the attainment of eternal happiness—and this cooperation is uncertain. God desires, therefore, that on the one hand we foster a certain anxiety in order that we may not, by trusting to our own strength, be put to confusion; but on the other hand He wishes us to be absolutely certain that it is His Will to make us eternally happy and that He will give us all the graces we need if we but ask Him. We should therefore trust with unwavering confidence in His goodness. St. Thomas says: "We must confidently expect eternal happiness from the power and mercy of God, believing firmly that God can make us happy and that He wishes to do so."

It sometimes happens that, owing to spiritual aridity or the disquiet resulting from a fault we have committed, we feel an absence of that sensible confidence in prayer which we would gladly experience. We must not on that account cease to pray, because God will very likely hear us sooner then than at other times, since we are apt to pray with greater distrust in ourselves and more hope in the goodness and fidelity of God. Oh how pleasing and acceptable it is to God when in fear and dread and every temptation we hope against hope; that is to say, when in spite of a feeling of mistrust arising from our own misery, we nevertheless trust in Him, as did the Patriarch Abraham, whom the Apostle praises because "against hope he believed in hope." (Rom. 4:18).

Secondly, our hope must be founded on God alone. The Lord forbids us to place our trust in creatures: "Put not your trust in princes." (Ps. 145:2). "Cursed be the man that trusteth in man." (Jer. 17:5). God desires us not to build on creatures because He does not want us to be attached to them with inordinate love. St. Vincent de Paul advises us not to count much on the protection of men, for if we do the Lord will withdraw from us; on the other hand, the more we grow in the love of God the more we will trust in Him. "I have run the way of thy commandments when thou didst enlarge my heart" (Ps. 118:32), by confidence.

But someone may say: If God alone is our hope, how can the Church address Mary as "Our hope"? Let us listen to what St. Thomas says on this point. We can place our hope in anyone, says the Saint, in a twofold manner; we can regard one as the principal and ultimate cause of our hope, or as the secondary and mediate cause. For example, one may hope for a favor from a king and from his minister or favorite. The king would be the principal or ultimate cause from which he hopes, the minister or favorite the mediate or intercessory. If the latter grants the favor, it comes nevertheless from the former, but through the intercession of the latter.

Now as the King of Heaven is Infinite Goodness itself, He desires to enrich us with His graces; but as great confidence on our part is necessary to obtain them, He has, in order to increase our confidence, given us His own Mother as our Mother and mediatrix to assist us. Therefore He wishes us to place our hope of salvation and of all goods and graces in her. According to the words of the prophet, they who put their trust in creatures are cursed. This passage refers to those who disregard their God and place their hope in the friendship and favor of man. But those who hope in Mary, the Mother of God, who has the power to obtain for them grace and eternal life, will be blessed by God. They give great joy to His loving heart, for He desires to see honored and loved that exalted creature who on earth loved and honored Him more than all men and angels together. We are right therefore in calling the Blessed Virgin our hope, for by means of her intercession we hope to obtain what we never could obtain by our feeble prayers alone. We beg her for her intercession, says Suarez, in order that the dignity of the intercessor may supply what is wanting in us. By invoking Mary with confidence, we manifest no distrust in the mercy of God, but simply fear on account of our own unworthiness. Holy Church is justified therefore in calling Mary "The Mother of holy hope," and by this she wishes to say that Mary awakens in us the hope of the inestimable goods of eternity.

Thirdly, our hope must be an active hope. In order that our hope may not be in vain it must labor; that is to say, to unbounded confidence in God we must unite the use of the means of salvation and sanctification which the Divine Majesty has given us; otherwise we should belong to those idle souls who tempt the Lord. We must act as if the obtaining of our salvation depended entirely on ourselves, and yet we must place all our confidence in God and be thoroughly convinced that of ourselves we are utterly unable to attain what we desire. God accomplishes everything by means of His grace, but He nevertheless desires our cooperation. If this cooperation, insignificant though it is, be wanting, God withdraws from us and treats us as indolent servants deserving of naught but to be cast out into exterior darkness. "Wherefore, brethren, labor the more, that by good works, you may make sure your calling and election." (2 Peter 1:10).

But what have we to do? Above all things we must pray. And how long must we pray? Until, says St. John Chrysostom, we hear the favorable sentence that assures us of eternal salvation. And he adds: He who says: "I will not stop praying until I am eternally happy," will certainly be eternally happy. "Know you not," says the Apostle, "that they that run in the race all run indeed, but one receiveth the prize? So run that you may obtain." (1 Cor. 9:24). In order to be eternally happy it is not enough, therefore, merely to pray; we must continue to pray until we are in possession of the crown that God has promised us.

If we desire to be happy for all eternity we must imitate David the prophet, who kept his eyes always directed to the Lord in order to implore His help and not be overcome by his enemies: "My eyes are ever towards the Lord, for he shall pluck my feet out of the snare." (Ps. 24:15). The devil is never tired of laying snares for our destruction: "Your adversary the devil, as a roaring lion, goeth about seeking whom he may devour." (1 Peter 5:8). Therefore we must keep our weapons ever in our hands to defend ourselves against such an enemy. We must say with the royal Psalmist: "I will pursue my enemies . . . until they are consumed." (Ps. 17:38). But how shall we win so important and difficult a victory? Only by prayer, says St. Augustine, and persevering prayer. But how long must it last? As long as the struggle goes on. Just as the contest never ceases, says St. Bonaventure, so we must never cease calling on God for His assistance, which is necessary for us so as not to succumb. "Woe to them that have lost patience," says the Wise Man (Ecclus. 2:16), and have given up prayer. Blessed shall we be "if we hold fast the confidence and glory of hope unto the end." (Heb. 3:6).

By means of the assistance we receive through prayer we must endeavor to keep the Commandments of God and do violence to ourselves so as not to yield to the temptations of Hell: "The kingdom of heaven suffereth violence and the violent bear it away." (Matt. 11:12). We must do violence to ourselves in temptations by conquering ourselves and mortifying our senses so as not to be overcome by the enemy of our souls. And when we have been guilty of a fault, says St. Ambrose, let us do violence to the Lord by prayers and tears in order to obtain His forgiveness. To inspire us with courage the Saint continues: "O blessed violence that God does not punish with His wrath but receives with mercy and reward! The greater this violence the more pleasing it is to Jesus Christ." He concludes with the following words: "We must rule over ourselves by subduing our evil passions in order to win Heaven which Jesus Christ has merited for us."

Chapter III

The Love of God

"Thou shalt love the Lord thy God with thy whole heart, and with thy whole soul, and with thy whole mind."—Matt. 22:37

Love of God is a divinely infused virtue which leads us to love the Lord Our God as the sovereign good, and purely for His own sake. The motive which prompts us to love God is His own boundless perfection, on account of which alone He deserves to be loved, even though we had no reward to hope for or no punishment to dread. He who loves God because he finds in Him his own happiness has an interested, a selfish love, which really belongs to the virtue of hope and not to love. But he who loves God because for His own sake He deserves to be loved, has the true and genuine love of friendship. The companions of King

Louis of France met a woman one day who carried in one hand a burning torch and in the other a vessel of water. On being asked what these things signified, she replied: "With this torch I would gladly burn Heaven, and with this water extinguish the fire of Hell, in order that men might love God not because of the reward of Heaven or the punishment of Hell, but simply and solely because He deserves to be loved."

The perfect love of God, however, does not exclude the hope of Heaven. We love God because He deserves to be loved, and we would love Him even though we had no reward to expect for doing so. But knowing as we do that He will give us a reward and that He even desires us to hope for it, we must confidently expect it and strive to attain it. To long for Heaven in order to possess God and love Him more perfectly is a true and perfect love of God, for eternal glory is the perfection of this love.

All perfection consists in the love of God; for love is the virtue which unites us most intimately with God. All the other virtues are of no account unless they are accompanied by love. On the other hand, love has all the other virtues in her train, according to the teaching of St. Paul: "Charity is patient, is kind: charity envieth not, dealeth not perversely; is not puffed up; is not ambitious, seeketh not her own, is not provoked to anger, thinketh no evil; rejoiceth not in iniquity, but rejoiceth with the truth; beareth all things, believeth all things, hopeth all things, endureth all things." (1 Cor. 13:4–7). "Love," concludes the Apostle, "is the fulfillment of the law." (Rom. 13:10). This induced St. Augustine to say: "Love and then do what you wish." He who loves another is very careful to cause him no offense; on the contrary, he is eager to do what will afford him pleasure. In like manner, he who loves God above all things abhors an offense against Him more than death itself, and strives as much as in him lies to please God. The first and greatest commandment which the Lord has given us, bids us love Him with our whole heart. "Thou shalt love the Lord thy God with thy whole heart." (Deut. 6:5). As God has loved us with an infinite love, He desires that we should love Him sincerely, and He longs to possess our whole heart: "Son, give me thy heart." (Prov. 23:26). "What doth the Lord, thy God, require of thee, but that thou fear the Lord, thy God, and walk in his ways and love him, and serve the Lord, thy God, with all thy heart and with all thy soul." (Deut. 10:12).

In the Old Law God commanded that fire be kept constantly burning on the altar. This altar, says

St. Gregory, is a type of our heart in which the fire of divine love must ever burn. Therefore, to the command to love Him with the whole heart, God added this injunction: "And these words which I command thee this day shall be in thy heart; and thou shalt meditate upon them sitting in thy house, and walking on thy journey, sleeping and rising. And thou shalt bind them as a sign on thy hand, and they shall be and shall move between thy eyes. And thou shalt write them in the entry and on the doors of thy house" (Deut. 6:6–9), in order to be continually mindful of them and make thy life conformable to them. As a reward for this love, God promises to give us Himself: "I am thy protector and thy reward exceeding great." (Gen. 15:1). The princes of this world reward their faithful subjects with possessions, honors and privileges. The Lord God gives them who love Him nothing less than Himself.

We should certainly be amply rewarded by the knowledge that God loves those who love Him, as He says in so many passages of Holy Writ: "I love them that love me." (Prov. 8:17). "He that abideth in charity, abideth in God and God in him." (1 John 4:16). "He that loveth me shall be loved by my Father; and I will love him." (John 14:21). If we knew that in some distant country there lived a handsome, holy, learned and compassionate prince, we could not refrain from loving him even though he had done us no good whatever. But what are all the excellent qualities of such a prince compared to those of our God! God possesses every perfection in an infinite degree. He possesses everything that makes Him worthy of our love. Could He have offered a greater, better, nobler, richer or more amiable object for our love than Himself?

Who is of higher nobility than God? Illustrious people are proud of the fact that their nobility goes back five hundred or a thousand years; the nobility of God is from all eternity. Who is greater than God? He is the Lord of all. The angels of Heaven and the powerful on earth are to Him as a drop in the mighty ocean or as a miserable grain of dust. A single word from Him brought the world into being; a single word could consign everything to oblivion. Who is richer than God? He possesses the treasures of Heaven and earth. Who is more beautiful than God? The beauty of all creatures vanishes before the glory of God. Who is more beneficent than God? St. Augustine says that the efforts of God to bestow favors on us are greater even than our desire to receive them. Who is more merciful than God? As soon as a sinner, though it be the most abandoned wretch on earth, humbles himself before

God and repents of his sins, God pardons him and receives him back. Who is more grateful than God? He never permits anything we do for love of Him to go unrewarded. In fine, who is more amiable and deserving of love than God? His very face fills the Saints of Heaven with a delight that constitutes their perfect happiness for all eternity. On the contrary, the greatest suffering of the reprobate consists in their knowing and seeing the lovable nature of God without being able to love Him.

We must therefore love God from our heart because He is worthy of all love. On account of the love God bears us, He is deserving of our sincerest gratitude. If we could unite the love of all men and angels and saints in one heart, this united love could not compare with the least degree of the love God bears each single soul. St. John Chrysostom says that God loves us more than we can love ourselves. "I have loved thee with an everlasting love" (Jer. 31:3), says God to each one of us. Those who loved us first on earth were our parents; but they began to love us only when they began to know us; God, on the contrary, loved us before we had an existence. Even before our parents lived, God loved us; yes, even before the creation of the world. In a word, He has loved us as long as He is God, and that is from all eternity. That heroic virgin St. Agnes was right when she said to those who sought to win her affections: "Another lover has come before you." O world and creatures of the world, I cannot love you; for as God has loved me first it is no more than right that I should give and consecrate to Him my heart.

NATURE BIDS US LOVE GOD

Heaven and earth cry out, says St. Augustine, everything I see speaks to me and urges me to love Thee my Lord; all creatures tell me Thou hast created them for love of me. When the Abbot de Rance, founder of the Trappists, would gaze through the window of his cell and see the stars and the heaven, the birds and the flowers, and consider that God had created all these to show him His love, he felt his heart inflamed with love for God. The very sight of a flower enkindled love in the heart of St. Mary Magdalen; "The loving God," she would exclaim, "has created this little flower to win my love."

When St. Teresa looked at the trees or flowers or the meadows and brooks, she said they accused her of ingratitude and chided her with her little love for a Creator who had called all these things into being just to be loved by her. "Greater love than this no man hath, that a man lay down his life for his friends." (John 15:13). Do you believe, O Christian soul, that Jesus Christ died for love of you? And if you believe this, can you love anything but Him? Before the Incarnation of the Eternal Word, says a celebrated author, man might doubt whether God loved him tenderly or not; but now that Jesus Christ has become man and died for us, such a doubt is impossible.

THE SUFFERINGS OF CHRIST A PROOF OF LOVE

How could Our Lord have better proved His love for us than by suffering so many pains and such contempt and by ending His life in bitter agony on the Cross? But alas, we have grown so accustomed to hear of the Incarnation and the Redemption, of a God born in a stable, a God that was scourged and crowned and crucified, that it makes but little impression on us. O holy faith, enlighten us that we may see what boundless love God has shown us in becoming man and dying on a cross. If Jesus Christ is not loved by mankind, it is because so few think of the love He has shown them; for would it be possible to think of this, and live without loving Him? St. Paul says: "The charity of Christ presseth us" (2 Cor. 5:14); that is to say, a soul that considers the love of Jesus for mankind is forced, as it were, to love in return.

When the Saints reflected on the Passion of our Blessed Redeemer they were so inflamed with love that they frequently gave vent to their astonishment and devotion. One day, in an ecstasy of devotion, St. Mary Magdalen de Pazzi caught hold of an image of the Crucified and exclaimed: "O Jesus, Thou hast become foolish with love. I say it and I shall never grow weary repeating it, love has made Thee foolish, my Jesus." If faith had not assured us of the truth of the great mystery of our Redemption, who could believe it possible that the Creator of the universe willed to suffer and die for His creatures. If Jesus had not died for us, who would ever have dared to ask God to become man and suffer and die to redeem mankind? Who would not have considered such a thought the height of folly? Indeed, when the heathens were told of the death of Jesus Christ they regarded it as a fable and called it an incredible folly, as St. Paul tells us: "We preach Christ crucified, unto the Jews indeed a stumbling block, and unto the Gentiles foolishness." (1 Cor. 1:23).

Yes, says St. Gregory, it seemed foolishness to them that the Author of life should die for men. How can we believe, they said, that a God who depends on no one and who in Himself is perfectly happy, should come down upon earth, assume human nature and die for His wretched creatures? That would be saying that for love of man God has become a fool. Yet it is a truth of our holy faith that for love of us poor ungrateful creatures, Jesus Christ, the true Son of God, gave Himself up to an ignominious death: "He hath loved us and delivered Himself for us." And why has Jesus done all this? He has done it, says St. Augustine, in order that man might recognize the inexpressible love which God bears him. Our Divine Redeemer Himself expressed the same idea in these words: "I have come to cast fire on the earth and what will I but that it be kindled!" (Luke 12:49). The fire of divine love I will kindle on earth and I desire nothing else but that the hearts of men be consumed with these holy flames.

With wonder and astonishment St. Bernard contemplates Our Lord bound like a criminal by the wicked soldiers. "O my Jesus," he exclaims, "how is it I see ropes and chains on Thy sacred body; art Thou not the King of Heaven and Holiness itself? It is we ungrateful servants who have deserved these ropes and chains." What has reduced Thee to such a pitiable condition, appearing like a wretched criminal? Ah, it is love. Love seems to forget its dignity when it seeks to win love in return. God, therefore, whom no man can vanquish, has been vanquished by love. His love for us induced Him to become man and to lose His life in a very ocean of suffering and sorrow.

As St. Bernard contemplates our Divine Redeemer before Pilate, he addresses Him in the following words: "Tell me, my beloved Jesus, Thou who art Innocence itself, what hast Thou done to deserve so cruel a sentence of death? Ah, I see now the cause of Thy death; I know what crime Thou hast committed, my Jesus! It is Thy love for us; yes, it is not Pilate, but Thy love that pronounces the sentence of death, and delivers the fatal blow." At the sight of a crucifix, St. Francis of Paul exclaimed: "O love, O love, O love!" And this is what we all must say at the sight of our crucified Lord: O love, O love, O love! Oh, that all men who look at the Cross of Christ would think of the love that God has borne each one of us! "With what love would we be inflamed," says St. Francis de Sales, "did we but see the flames of love that burn in the heart of Christ! What a happiness for us did we glow with the fire that consumes our Lord and God! What joy, to be bound with the bonds of love for God!" As St. Bonaventure has said, the wounds of our Saviour must move the most unfeeling hearts and warm the coldest souls with love.

How many are the darts of love that issue from these sacred wounds and pierce the hardest hearts! "What is man," says Job, "that thou shouldst magnify him? or why dost thou set thy heart upon him?" (Job 7:17). O my God, what is wretched man that Thou shouldst honor him so much? What good hast Thou ever received from him, that Thou shouldst be wholly intent, as it seems, upon bestowing benefits on him and showing him Thy love? St. Thomas says that the love which consumes the heart of God makes it appear as though in man He saw His God, and that He could not be happy unless man were happy too.

Truly, Christian soul, if you had been God could Jesus Christ have done more for you than He has done by His life of suffering and His ignominious death? And if there had been a question of our Redeemer saving the life of His own Eternal Father, could He have done more than He has done for you? But, O God, where is our gratitude? If an insignificant servant had suffered for us what our heavenly Spouse has endured, could we ever forget it? Could we live without loving him? In very truth, we ought to be fairly beside ourselves with love when reflecting on the death of Jesus Christ, and say with St. Paschal: "My Love is nailed to the Cross for me; my Love has died for me."

But what we have neglected to do in the past we can at least try to do in the future, as God still gives us time. Jesus died for us, says St. Paul, in order that His love might win a perfect mastery over our hearts: "For to this end Christ died and rose again; that he might be Lord both of the dead and of the living." (Rom. 14:9). "And Christ died for all," says the same Apostle, "that they also who live, may not now live to themselves, but unto him who died for them and rose again." (2 Cor. 5:15). With this intention of the Divine Redeemer the Saints have corresponded most perfectly. When considering the love that induced their Lord to suffer and die for them, they deemed it but little, for love of Him, to offer Him all they had, yes, even their very lives.

How many potentates, kings, queens and empresses have renounced their riches and relatives and given up their throne and country to enter a cloister and devote their lives to the love of Jesus Christ! How many martyrs have considered it a source of joy and happiness to surrender their lives in the midst of cruel torments for the love of their Lord and God! How many young men and women have rejected the most brilliant alliances and have gladly offered their lives as a token of their love for a God who died for love of them!

And you, Christian soul, what have you done for your Divine Redeemer! What proof of your love have you given Him? It is certain that Jesus died for you as well as for a St. Lucy, a St. Agatha, a St. Agnes. Think of the special graces He has given you and which He has denied to so many others. Think of the many He has permitted to be born in countries where infidelity and unbelief hold sway! How many of these unhappy creatures deprived of the Sacraments and means of eternal salvation are consigned to eternal perdition! And you have received the grace to be born in the bosom of the Church of God! Think of the great mercy that God has shown you, forgiving the many offenses you have committed against Him. To move Him to forgive you, all that was necessary was to repent and to ask for forgiveness; but, alas, you have treated Him with ingratitude and offended Him anew. And yet He was willing to pardon you again and with the same love. Instead of punishing you as you deserved, He showered upon you His graces and inspirations. At this very moment, while you are reading these words, He continues to invite you to His love. Well then! What do you propose to do? Is it possible you can resist any longer? Why do you still hesitate? Do you wish to wait until God ceases to call, and abandons you?

MEANS OF ADVANCING IN GOD'S LOVE

We shall now consider the means of advancing in the love of God. St. Teresa says that it is an extraordinary grace for a soul to be called to the perfect love of God. To these happy souls, you, dear reader, belong. In order, however, to dedicate yourself entirely to the love of your Divine Spouse, as He desires you to do, you must courageously make use of the means conducive to that end. The first means is an ardent desire for this perfect love. With such a desire you have already taken a considerable step. God distributes His graces in abundance to those only who hunger and thirst for them, as the Blessed Virgin says in her wonderful hymn of praise, the Magnificat: "He hath filled the hungry with good things." (Luke 1:53). But this desire is absolutely necessary for us, for otherwise we should never persevere in our efforts to obtain the treasure of the love of God. We take little or no pains in striving to obtain that for which we have little or no desire. On the other hand, all trouble is light and sweet when our efforts are prompted by an ardent desire. Hence it is that Our Lord calls those blessed who have not merely a desire, but a hunger—that is to say, a great desire—for holiness: "Blessed are they who hunger and thirst after justice." (Matt. 5:6).

The second means of obtaining the perfect love of God consists in renouncing all love that does not refer to God. God desires to possess our hearts alone and will tolerate no rival. St. Augustine relates that the Roman Senate willingly acknowledged the 30,000 gods of the pagans, while they refused to worship the God of the Christians, because He was a jealous God who wished to be adored alone. Our God was right in claiming exclusive adoration, because He alone is the only true God. Accordingly, if we wish to arrive at the perfect love of God, we must banish from our heart every attachment that has not God for its object. The ardent St. Francis de Sales said: "If I knew that in my heart there was a single fiber that was not from God, in God, and for God, I would immediately tear it out." As long as the heart is not free from earthly inclinations, the love of God can find no entrance there; but as soon as it is detached from creatures the fire of divine love is enkindled and grows continually stronger. Therefore St. Teresa used to say: "Separate your heart from creatures and seek God; you will surely find Him then." Father Segneri the Younger wrote one day to a pious friend: "Divine love is a beneficent robber who takes from us all earthly inclinations, so that the soul can say to her beloved Spouse: What do I wish but Thee alone." St. Francis de Sales expresses himself in a similar manner: "The pure love of God consumes in the heart all that is not God, to turn everything into love, for all that man does for God is love."

"I count all things but as dung," says St. Paul, "that I may gain Christ." (Phil. 3:8). When the love of God has entered our hearts, we place no longer any value on what the world esteems: "If a man shall give all the substance of his house for love, he shall despise it as nothing." (Cant. 8:7). "If a house is on fire," says St. Francis de Sales, "they throw everything out the window." As soon as a heart is inflamed with the love of God it seeks to divest itself of everything earthly so as to love nothing but God. Does God ask too much when He desires the soul to love nothing but Him? "No," says St. Bonaventure, "God is infinitely amiable and supremely good, deserving of our undivided love; He is perfectly right when He desires that a heart which He has created, should belong to Him alone; and since He has given Himself in sacrifice for us, He has acquired a still greater claim to our undivided love."

SELF-DENIAL

In order to attain to the perfect love of God it is necessary, moreover, to deny oneself by gladly embracing what is opposed to self-love, and refusing oneself what self-love demands. One day when St. Teresa was sick, they brought her a very palatable dish; the Saint would not touch it. The attendant urged her to eat, saying that the dish was well-prepared. "That's just the reason I abstain from eating it," replied the Saint. And so with us; what pleases us most, in that we must deny ourselves, and just because it pleases us. For example, we must turn our eyes away from this or that object because it is beautiful; deny ourselves this or that pleasure because it is most agreeable to us; do a service to an ungrateful person just because he is ungrateful; take a bitter medicine just because it is bitter. According to St. Francis de Sales, our self-love wants to have a share in everything, even in things the most holy. For this very reason, says the Saint, we must love even virtue without attachment. For example, it is necessary to love prayer and solitude; but when obedience or charity prevent us from devoting ourselves to prayer and solitude we should not be disquieted, but accept resignedly everything that happens by the will of God to thwart our inclinations.

THE PASSION OF CHRIST

The fourth means of acquiring the perfect love of God consists in frequent meditation on the sufferings of Jesus Christ. St. Mary Magdalen de Pazzi says that he who has given himself entirely to the love of his Crucified Lord needs but to look at the cross to be buried in the contemplation of the boundless love that Jesus Christ has borne him. It would seem as though our Redeemer endured so many different torments and insults, such as His betrayal, His agony, His scourging, His crowning and His Crucifixion in order to afford subjects for meditation to those souls that love Him. And yet we must not reflect on the sufferings of Jesus Christ for the sake of the consolation and sweetness it affords, but only to inflame our hearts with love for our suffering Saviour and to learn from Him what He desires us to do.

At the same time, we must declare ourselves ready to bear everything patiently for love of Him who suffered so much for love of us. The Lord once revealed to a pious hermit that no devotion was better calculated to enkindle the love of God in the heart than meditation on the sufferings of Christ. It has always been a favorite devotion with the Saints. St. Francis of Assisi became a seraph of love by meditating on the Passion of Christ. He was found one day bathed in tears and uttering loud sighs. When asked what was the cause of his grief he replied: "I am weeping over the pains and insults of my Divine Master. But what grieves me most is that men for whom He suffered so much never think of the torments He endured." If the Saint heard the bleating of a lamb, or saw anything that reminded him of the sufferings of Christ, he was forced to shed tears. Once when he was sick and someone advised him to read an edifying book, he replied: "My book is Jesus Crucified." He constantly exhorted his brethren to think of the Passion of Christ.

The fifth means of acquiring the treasure of God's love is prayer. The constant prayer of a Christian soul must be: "Jesus, give me Thy holy love; Mary my Mother, obtain for me the love of God; my Guardian

Angel and all my holy patrons, intercede for me that I may love my God with my whole heart and soul." The Lord is generous in the bestowal of His gifts; but He is especially bountiful in giving His love to those who seek it.

Chapter IV

Love for our Neighbor

"This is my commandment, that you love one another as I have loved you."—John 15:12

It is impossible to love the Lord our God without at the same time loving our neighbor. The commandment that obliges us to love our God, obliges us also to love our neighbor. "And this commandment we have from God, that he who loveth God, love also his brother." (1 John 4:21). From these words of the Apostle, St. Thomas Aquinas concludes that the one virtue of love embraces the love of God and the love of our neighbor. St. Jerome tells us that when the disciples of St. John the Evangelist asked him why he spoke so often of brotherly love, he replied: "Because it is the commandment of the Lord, and the fulfillment of this alone is sufficient for eternal salvation."

St. Catherine of Genoa once said to Our Lord: "O my God, Thou commandest me to love my neighbor, and I can love no one but Thee." Our Saviour replied: "My daughter, whoever loves Me loves everything that is loved by Me." Why, therefore, must we love our neighbor? Because he is loved by God. St. John was therefore right when he called him a liar who says that he loves God but hates his neighbor. Our Lord has promised that He will regard as done to Himself what we do for the least of our brethren: "Amen I say to you, as long as you did it to one of these, my least brethren, you did it to me." (Matt. 25:40). From this St. Catherine of Genoa concludes: "If you wish to know how much a person loves his God, see how much he loves his neighbor."

Christian charity is one of the principal fruits of the Redemption. The prophet Isaias had foretold this truth in the following words: "The wolf shall dwell with the lamb, and the leopard shall lie down with the kid: the calf and the lion and the sheep shall abide together, and a little child shall lead them." (Is. 11:6). By these words he wished to say that the followers of Jesus Christ, though from different nations and different climes and of unlike characters and inclinations, would nevertheless live peacefully together, for brotherly love would induce them to practice mutual forbearance. And St. Luke, when speaking of the first Christians, says: "The multitude of believers had but one heart and one soul." (Acts 4:32).

This was the effect of the prayer which our Redeemer addressed to His heavenly Father on the eve of His Sacred Passion: "Holy Father, keep them in thy name whom thou hast given me; that they may be one, as we also are." (John 17:11).

RASH JUDGMENTS

Dear Christian reader, if you are desirous of practicing the beautiful virtue of charity, strive in the first place to reject every rash judgment, every distrust, and unfounded suspicion of your neighbor. It is a grave fault, without sufficient reason, to doubt the innocence of another. It is graver still to entertain a real suspicion, and far more so when without adequate reason we hold for certain that another has done wrong. He who judges in this manner will himself be judged: "Judge not," says our Divine Redeemer, "that you may not be judged; for with what judgment you judge, you shall be judged; and with what measure you mete, it shall be measured to you again." (Malt. 7:1–2). I say, "without sufficient reason," for when there are good grounds for suspecting or even believing evil of another, no sin is committed by such thoughts. However, it is, according to the teaching of the Apostle, always safer and more in harmony with charity to think well of others and to refrain from all unfavorable judgments and suspicions: "Charity thinketh no evil." (1 Cor. 13:5).

This advice is not intended, of course, for those who are entrusted with the guidance of others, for it is advisable and even at times necessary for such to entertain a certain distrust; otherwise great evils may arise as the result of an overweening confidence. But if you are not charged with the duty of watching over others, try always to think well of your fellow men. St. Jane de Chantal says: "In our neighbor we must direct our attention to the good and not to the evil. And if it should happen that we deceive ourselves by regarding as good what in reality is bad, we need not be disturbed, for St. Augustine says, charity is not grieved when by mistake it attributes something good to one who is evil."

Beware of trying to find out the faults of your neighbor. Do not imitate those who go about inquiring what is said of them and thereby fill their heart with suspicion, bitterness and aversion. Things are often represented to be different from what they really are. If you hear, therefore, that an unfavorable comment has been passed on you, do not attach much importance to the assertion and do not seek to know its origin or source. Act in such a manner that everyone must speak well of you, and then let others talk as they will. You might possibly say to yourself when your faults are spoken of: "That is the least they can say about me; what if they knew all!"

CALUMNY AND SLANDER

To practice charity in speech you must, above all things, avoid calumny and slander. He who has contracted this deplorable habit disfigures his own soul and is hated everywhere, as the Holy Ghost says: "He shall defile his own soul and shall be hated by all." (Ecclus. 21:31). If there are some who agree with him at times and encourage him in speaking ill of his neighbor, these very persons will later avoid him and be on their guard against his venomous tongue. They reason, and justly so, that if he speaks ill of others to them, he will speak ill of them to others. St. Jerome remarks that many who have renounced the other vices seem not to be able to keep from uncharitable talk. Even among those who have vowed to strive after perfection there are many who cannot move their tongue without wounding someone. God grant they may not end their life as did one unhappy slanderer; when on his deathbed, he bit his tongue in a fit of rage, and in this condition he died. St. Bernard speaks of another who was about to speak ill of St. Malachy when suddenly his tongue became swollen and was devoured by worms; after seven days of terrible agony he died a wretched death.

But, on the other hand, how dear to God and man is he who speaks well of everyone! "If in the course of his life, a man never spoke ill of his fellowman, I would consider him a saint," says St. Mary Magdalen de Pazzi. Carefully guard against the habit of speaking unkindly of others, and especially of superiors. We render ourselves guilty of detraction not only when we reveal the hidden faults of our neighbor, but also when we interpret his good works amiss or assign to them an evil intention. It is a common fault with some people when speaking of their neighbor to begin with praise and end with blame. For example, "So and So is very capable; isn't it too bad he's so proud?" Or, "He is very generous, but he spoils it all by being revengeful."

Dear reader, try always to say only what is good of your neighbor. Speak of others as you would wish others to speak of you. And in regard to the absent, follow the beautiful advice of St. Mary Magdalen of Pazzi: "Say nothing of an absent brother that you would not wish to say in his presence." When you hear others speaking unkindly, be careful not to encourage them by manifesting an interest or pleasure in what they say; you might otherwise be a partner in their guilt.

"Six things there are," says the Wise Man, "which the Lord hateth and the seventh his soul detesteth." (Prov. 6:16). This seventh thing is the person who "soweth discord among brethren." The talebearer goes about telling people what he has heard others say of them. He scatters the seeds of discord, enmity, quarrels and revenge. How severe the account such tongues will have to give before the judgment seat of God. If in the heat of passion one person speaks ill of another, we can have patience with him; most likely he will repent of what he has said. But how can the Lord be patient with those who deliberately sow seeds of discord and strife and destroy the peace and happiness of their fellow men? "Hast thou heard a word against thy neighbor?" says the Holy Ghost; "let it die within thee, trusting that it will not burst thee." (Ecclus. 19:10). You must not be satisfied merely to enclose it in your heart; you must let it die there.

There are people who, on hearing a secret, seem to suffer the agonies of death until they can make it known in some way. Their secret is like a thorn that is piercing the heart and it must be torn out as soon as possible. Do not act in this way. If you know that your neighbor has committed a fault, be silent about it. Only then, when the good of others or of the guilty one demands it, may you reveal what you know.

In conversation, as far as possible avoid disputes. There are some people who have such a spirit of contradiction that they seem to take pleasure in always questioning what others say, even though it be of little or no importance. Thus little trifles sometimes give rise to a war of words; charity is wounded and the bonds of friendship are broken beyond repair. "Strive not in a matter which doth not concern thee," says the Wise Man. (Ecclus. 11:9).

But, you will say: "I am right; I cannot bear to hear such absurd talk." Listen to what Cardinal Bellarmine says: "An ounce of charity is better than tons of right." To yield in a war of words is to win a victory, for you grow in virtue and preserve peace, which is better far than obstinately maintaining your right.

When you are offended or spoken to in an angry way, try to reply with meekness. If you are too agitated to do so it is better to say nothing at all, for in the heat of passion you may think what you say is right and proper, but afterwards, when the excitement has passed away, you will regret what you have said. An eye that is disturbed by anger, says St. Bernard, cannot see what is right or wrong. Passion is like a black veil that is drawn before the eyes; while it is there we cannot see things in their proper light. When he who offends you asks pardon, be generous enough to grant it in a gracious manner. If you have offended another be quick to repair the harm you have done. St. Bernard says, the best way to heal the wound you have inflicted by uncharitableness is to humble yourself. The longer you delay, the harder it becomes, and eventually you may neglect it altogether. Our Blessed Saviour once said: "If thou offer thy gift at the altar, and there thou remember that thy brother hath anything against thee; leave thy offering before the altar, and go first to be reconciled to thy brother: and then coming thou shalt offer thy gift." (Matt. 5:23). But if it should happen that such self-humiliation would only anger the offended person the more, endeavor by some other means to quiet him.

ALMSGIVING

A very important duty of charity towards our neighbor consists in giving him alms when he is poor and needy and we ourselves are in a position to do so: "Of that which remaineth, give alms," says our Blessed Redeemer. (Luke 11:41). But we must distinguish: If our neighbor is in extreme want we are bound to assist him with what is not absolutely necessary for our own sustenance. If his necessity is not extreme, but very great, we must help him with what we ourselves do not need. "Alms delivereth from death," said the Archangel Raphael to Tobias, "and the same is that which purgeth away sins, and maketh to find mercy and life everlasting." (Tob. 12:9).

"He that hath mercy on the poor," says the Holy Ghost, "lendeth to the Lord; and he will repay him." (Prov. 19:17). If we can do nothing else let us at least recommend him to God, for prayer is also an alms. "He that shall see his brother in need," says St. John, "and shall shut up his heart against him, how doth the charity of God abide in him?" (1 John 3:17). "With what measure you mete it shall be measured to you again," says our Blessed Redeemer. (Matt. 7:2). St. Mary Magdalen de Pazzi said she would feel happier by assisting her neighbor than if she were raised to heavenly contemplation: "If I am in contemplation," said she, "God is helping me; if I assist my neighbor I am helping God." This is very true, for Our Lord Himself said: "Whatsoever you do to the least of my brethren you do to me." (Matt. 25:40).

LOVE YOUR ENEMIES

Above all things I would recommend to you charity towards your enemies. "Love your enemies," says Our Lord, "do good to them that hate you; and pray for them that persecute and calumniate you, that you may be the children of your Father who is in heaven." (Matt. 5:44). How sad it is to see Christians who go to church and even to Holy Communion and still retain enmity in their hearts! If anyone has injured you, and you wish to be revenged, try to act as the Saints have done. St. Paulinus tells us that to love one's enemy is a heavenly revenge. St. Catherine of Siena took revenge on a woman who had attacked her honor, and this was her revenge: During a long and severe illness which the woman suffered, St. Catherine waited on her as a servant. St. Acacius sold his possessions in order to assist a man who had robbed him of his good name. St.

Ambrose supported a man who had made an attempt on his life. Venustian, the Governor of Umbria, a persecutor of the Church, had the hands of St. Sabinus, Bishop of Spoleto, cut off because the Saint, instead of adoring an idol, broke it to pieces. Hereupon, the Governor was seized with such violent pains in the eyes that he called on the Saint to help him. Sabinus prayed for him and not only cured his body but also his soul; the Governor embraced the True Faith.

St. Chrysostom relates the following example. When St. Meletius, Patriarch of Antioch, saw the people about to stone the officer who was leading him into exile, the Saint stretched out his arms and embraced him, thus saving his life. But someone will say: "These were saints; I have no such strength and grace." St. Ambrose replies: "If strength is wanting, pray to God and He will give it you." If we forgive others, we are certain of forgiveness ourselves: "Forgive and you will be forgiven," says Our Lord. (Luke 6:37). "If I called a dead person to life," says St. Baptist Verani, "I would be less certain of being loved by God than when I am prepared to do good to him who has done evil to me." Our Lord Himself said one day to St. Angela de Foligno: "The surest sign of mutual love between Me and

My servants consists in their loving someone who has offended them."

If you can do nothing else, dear reader, pray for those who have offended or injured you. Her sisters in religion used to say of St. Joanna of the Cross: "If you want Mother Joanna to pray for you, all that is necessary is to offend her." One day when St. Elizabeth, Queen of Hungary, was praying for a person who had injured her, she heard Our Lord say: "You have never uttered a prayer that was more agreeable to Me than this; in consequence I forgive you all your sins."

The love that is directed to the spiritual welfare of your neighbor is doubtless the best. In the eyes of God, says St. Bernard, a soul is worth more than the whole world. Could there be anything, therefore, more noble and sublime than to labor with Jesus Christ for the salvation of souls? But you may say: "I am not called to the service of the sanctuary; this is the work of the priests." St. Augustine replies: "If you truly love God, you will do all in your power to make others love Him." We may likewise say: If you truly love yourself, you will make every possible effort to win souls to God, for he who converts a sinner saves not only the sinner, but himself. When Jonathan with great danger to himself had delivered the Jews from the hands of the Philistines, he was condemned to death by his father because, in spite of a prohibition, he had eaten a little honey. But the people said to Saul: "Should Jonathan, who has delivered us all from death, himself die?" In this way they obtained his pardon and deliverance from death.

In a similar manner the souls that we help to save will plead beseechingly in our behalf before the judgment seat of God. And God will answer their pleading: "From henceforth they may rest from their labors, for their works follow them." (Apoc. 14:13). St. Gregory says we shall gain as many crowns as we win souls to God. "So let your light shine before men that they may see your good works and glorify your Father who is in heaven." (Matt. 5:16). Our Lord said one day to St. Mary Magdalen de Pazzi: "See how many Christians are in the hands of the devil; if My elect do not free them by prayer, these unfortunates will be eternally lost."

If you have an opportunity to assist the dying, remember that you are performing an act of charity very acceptable to God. St. Philip Neri often saw the angels putting words of consolation on the tongues of those who assisted the dying. See that the priest is called in time to administer the last Sacraments while the patient is still conscious. Suggest little acts of faith, hope, love and contrition. Assist the sufferer to pronounce the holy Names very often and to make acts of resignation to the Will of God. When the soul is departing, say the prayers for the dying and recommend the departed soul when it appears before the judgment seat of God. An evergreen wreath of prayers should be laid on the grave and frequent mementoes made during Holy Mass for a speedy entrance of the departed soul into the everlasting joys of our heavenly home.

Chapter V

Poverty and Detachment

"Blessed are the poor in spirit, for theirs is the kingdom of heaven."—Matt. 5:3

When the masters of the spiritual life speak of poverty in spirit, they generally understand it in a twofold sense. In the restricted sense it means a detachment of the heart from earthly possessions. In the broad sense, by poverty in spirit they mean detachment from everything earthly, no matter what it may be. In this sense, poverty in spirit is necessary for all who are striving after perfection.

Our heart cannot exist without love; it will either love God or creatures. If it does not love creatures, it certainly will love God. In order to become holy we must therefore banish from our heart all that is not for God. When anyone came to the Fathers of the desert and desired to be received by them he was asked: "Do you bring an empty heart that it may be filled by the Holy Ghost?" And they were right, for a heart that is filled with the things of earth has no room for the love of God. He who brings a vessel filled with earth to the spring will never be able to fill it with water until he empties it of the earth with which it is filled. How does it happen that so many pray and go frequently to Holy Communion, and still make no considerable progress in the love of God? The reason is doubtless because the heart is full of self-esteem, of vanity, self-will and attachment to creatures. He, therefore, who wishes to arrive at the perfect love of God must practice poverty in spirit. He must be detached from worldly possessions, from temporal honors, from his fellow creatures and from himself.

Our Divine Redeemer has said: "Blessed are the poor in spirit, for theirs is the kingdom of heaven." (Matt. 5:3). And again: "Woe to you rich." (Luke 6:24). What does He mean by these words? Does He mean that all the poor are happy and all the rich unhappy? Certainly not; He wishes rather to exhort all, both rich and poor, to the practice of the virtue of poverty and detachment. For there are many who are poor in the goods of this world, but their hearts cling tenaciously to the things of earth; while on the other hand, there are wealthy people whose hearts are entirely detached from their earthly possessions.

THE POOR IN SPIRIT

The poor of this world do not possess poverty of spirit from the mere fact that they suffer the want of the goods of this life. Poverty of spirit consists in the desire to possess nothing but God. "I meet a poor man," says St. Augustine, "and yet I find he is not poor"; that is to say: Many are poor in reality, few in spirit and desire. St. Teresa says that they who appear externally poor without being so in spirit deceive both the world and themselves. What will their poverty in possession avail them? He who is externally poor, but in his heart has an insatiable desire for wealth has only the burdens, but not the virtue of poverty. The truly virtuous poor desire nothing but God, and for that very reason they are immensely rich. Of them St. Paul speaks when he says: "Having nothing, they possess all things." (2 Cor. 6:10).

But how can they who are rich in the goods of this earth still possess poverty in spirit? They can do so by having no inordinate attachment to their riches. What are the goods of this earth? They are really goods only in appearance that can never satisfy the heart of man. "You have eaten," says the prophet Aggeus, "but you have not had enough." (Agg. 1:6). Instead of satisfying the hunger, says St. Bernard, they only increase it. If worldly goods could satisfy the heart of man, the rich and the mighty would be perfectly happy; but experience teaches the contrary. As a rule they are the most unhappy of men, for they are tortured by fears, jealousies and sadness. "Vanity of vanities and all is vanity." I have had all these things, said Solomon, "and behold all is vanity and vexation of spirit." (Eccles. 1:14).

Add to this the fact that those who are always intent upon increasing their earthly possessions are in great danger of being eternally lost. The Apostle warns us against this in his epistle to Timothy: "They that will become rich, fall into temptation and into the snare of the devil, and into many unprofitable and hurtful desires which drown men in destruction and perdition. For the desire of money is the root of all evils; which some coveting have erred from the faith, and have entangled themselves in many sorrows." (1 Tim. 6:9–10).

If we desire to belong to God, we must renounce all attachment to the goods of earth. He who strives for earthly goods, says St. Philip Neri, will never become a saint. The riches we must strive to gain, says St. Prosper, are not temporal goods but virtues, humility, meekness, chastity, piety, for these will constitute our greatness and glory in Heaven. "Lay not up to yourselves treasures on earth: where the rust and moth consume, and where thieves break through and steal." (Matt. 6:19). The wealthy can practice poverty in spirit by giving alms and performing good works. "O happy exchange," says St. Peter Damian, "we give earth and receive gold"; that is to say, we give our earthly possessions and receive in return graces from God and an eternal reward in Heaven. In all ages of the Christian era there have been people of distinguished rank who lived in great simplicity in order to be able to perform good works. Violanta Palombara, a lady of the nobility, clothed herself in ordinary linen. Her rosary was made of cheap wood. Just before her death she was heard to exclaim: "Oh, what do I see! My dress is become brilliant and my beads are sparkling like diamonds."

TRUE DETACHMENT

Our detachment from the things of this earth is proved by our resignation to the Will of God in temporal disasters, such as financial loss by accident or theft. Faith teaches us that nothing happens without the permission of God. If, therefore, we suffer the loss of our good name or our temporal possessions, God does not of course will the sin that is thereby committed, but He wills or permits the suffering that falls to our lot and He wills it for our good. When a messenger came to the pious Job and announced that the Sabeans had stolen all his belongings and murdered his children, the holy man replied: "The Lord gave, and the Lord hath taken away." He did not say: "The Lord gave and the Sabeans have taken away," but: "The Lord gave and the Lord hath taken away: as it hath pleased the Lord, so is it done: blessed be the name of the Lord." (Job 1:21). Finally, we prove to evidence that we possess the spirit of detachment when we are ready to sacrifice everything we have—riches, honors, dignities, position—in short, every temporal advantage, rather than offend God.

Such were the sentiments of the holy martyrs. Dacian, the Governor of the Province of Tanigma, addressed the young deacon Vincent in the following words: "My boy, you are still young; the smiles and favors of fortune await you. To possess them, all you need do is to renounce your religion; obey the Emperor and escape an ignominious death." Vincent turned to Bishop Valerius, who with him stood before the Governor, and said: "My Father, if you wish, I shall answer for you too." The holy Bishop, who stood prepared to suffer everything for the love of Jesus Christ, replied: "Yes, my son; as I have already commissioned you to preach the word of God, now I commission you to confess our faith." Hereupon Vincent declared to the Governor that both Valerius and himself adored but one God and that they could not and would not adore devils, for such were the gods of the Roman empire. "Moreover," he said, "do not imagine you will influence us by threats or promises. There is nothing in this world to compare with the honor and the happiness of dying for Jesus Christ." Enraged at this fearlessness of the holy deacon, the Governor cried out: "Either sacrifice to the gods or your contempt will cost you your lives." The holy deacon replied with a loud voice: "I have already told you that you could do us no greater favor than to put us to death for Jesus Christ, and you may rest assured that you will grow weary torturing us before we are tired of being tormented."

Let us now consider some of the means that are necessary for acquiring this detachment from the things of earth. In the first place, to remove all inordinate attachment from the heart it is necessary to dwell on the thought of death. The day of death is called "the day of loss" because on this day the riches and honors and pleasures of earth are lost. On this account, says St. Ambrose, we should not really call these things our own because we cannot bring them with us into the next world, where only virtue can accompany us. That man was right therefore who, when realizing the vanity of the world, wrote on a skull the following words: "To one who thinks, everything here below seems deserving of contempt." But why are there so many unhappy lovers of this earth? Because there are so few who think of death.

Poor children of Adam, says the Holy Ghost, why do you not banish from your hearts all earthly attachment? "Why do you love vanity and seek after lying?" (Ps. 4:3). What happened to your forefathers will happen to you. They too loved the dwelling that is now yours; now they are no more; they have gone into eternity, and you shall follow them.

THE POVERTY OF CHRIST

The second means consists in frequent meditation on the poverty of Jesus Christ and the esteem which He had for this holy virtue. For our good, and in order to give us an example, our Divine Redeemer wished to lead so poor a life on earth that St. Mary Magdalen de Pazzi called poverty the spouse of Jesus Christ. St. Bernard says: "Poverty was not to be found in Heaven, but it reigned on earth. Mankind, however, did not recognize its worth, and therefore the Son of God came down to choose poverty for His inseparable companion and to teach us to esteem it."

This thought is in keeping with what the Apostle writes to his disciples: "For you know the grace of our Lord Jesus Christ, that being rich he became poor for your sakes; that through his poverty you might be rich." (2 Cor. 8:9). Although our Divine Redeemer was the Lord and Master of all the riches of Heaven and earth, He willed nevertheless to become poor in this world that through His example we might become rich. He wished to induce us to love poverty as He did, for poverty, by detaching us from earthly riches, enables us to share in the treasures of Heaven. The third means consists in frequently dwelling upon the teaching of our Blessed Lord that the poor in spirit shall have a great and certain reward. Their reward is certain, for when our Saviour enumerated the Beatitudes in the Gospel, He referred in most instances to the future, as "Blessed are the meek for they shall possess the land! Blessed are the pure of heart for they shall see God!" But to the poor in spirit He promises happiness even in this life: "Blessed are the poor in spirit for theirs is the kingdom of heaven." (Matt. 5:3). While here on earth, they receive special graces.

The reward of the poor in spirit is, secondly, very great. "The less we have here," says St. Teresa, "the greater will be our joy in Heaven, where our dwelling shall correspond to the love with which we imitated the life of poverty of our Divine Master here on earth." The truly poor in spirit enjoy a heavenly peace even here in this world. "Oh what happiness voluntary poverty bestows," says St. Lawrence Justinian; "the poor man possesses nothing and therefore has nothing to fear; he is always cheerful, for he always has an abundance, since he knows how to draw spiritual gain out of everything that is burdensome." According to the words of St. Bernard, a miser craves for riches like a beggar, because he can never satisfy his insatiable desire. He, on the other hand, who is poor from choice despises the possessions of this earth and is at the same time the master of all.

The fourth means consists in loving God without reserve. A soul that is thoroughly penetrated with divine love is inclined of itself, of course not without the aid of grace, to divest itself of all earthly things which might prevent it from belonging entirely to God. For the love of Jesus Christ, a certain rich man had renounced all his possessions. When one of his friends asked him how he had fallen into such poverty, he drew forth a copy of the Gospel and said: "This is what has robbed me of all I possessed." The Holy Ghost tells us that all the treasures of earth are as nothing in the eyes of one who loves God. If a soul directs all its love to God, that soul despises riches, pleasures, honors, kingdoms and everything else this world can give. It loves only God, and says without intermission: "O my God, Thee alone do I desire!" He who loves God is not anxious to gain the esteem and love of men; all his efforts are directed to one end, to please God, the only object of his love.

St. Hilary says: "All earthly honors are things of the devil." Indeed, the devil is working in the interest of Hell when he inspires a soul with a desire for the esteem of the world. For when a soul loses humility it runs the risk of being hurled into the abyss. A great servant of God once said: "When we hear that a Solomon, or a Tertullian, these cedars of Lebanon have fallen, we have a proof that they did not give themselves entirely to God, but nourished pride in their heart, and on that account strayed from the path of righteousness. We should tremble when we experience within ourselves the desire to shine before others and to be honored by them. Such promptings may be the beginning of our eternal misery." Many who have pretensions to piety are adorers of their own honor. They have a certain appearance of virtue, and at the same time a desire to be praised for all they do. If no one praises them, they praise themselves. They wish to appear better than others, and if they hear that their good name has been assailed, they lose all control of themselves, neglect Holy Communion and all their exercises of piety. They can find no rest until they have made good the supposed injury done to them.

Such is not the conduct of those who love God sincerely. Far from praising themselves or taking pleasure in hearing themselves praised, they are disturbed on account of the recognition they receive, and they rejoice when they are called upon to suffer contempt. "I am only that which I am before God," said St. Francis of Assisi. Of what use is it to be esteemed by men if we are contemptible in the sight of God? And what does it matter if we are despised by the world, provided we are acceptable before God? "He who praises us," says St. Augustine, "does not free us from the punishment we have deserved for our sins, and he who blames us is not able to rob us of the merit of our good works."

"O my God," exclaims St. Teresa, "what matters it whether we are loved or hated by creatures, provided we are without blame before Thee!" The only desire of the Saints was to live in obscurity and contempt. "What harm do they do us who have a bad opinion of us?" asks St. Francis de Sales. "Should not we have just such an opinion of ourselves? Is it right to wish others to think well of us, when we know very well that we are wicked?"

A HIDDEN LIFE

A hidden and obscure life affords great security to those who sincerely desire to love God. Our Divine Master Himself deigned to teach us this by His own example, for He spent 30 years in the obscurity of Nazareth and the workshop of a humble carpenter. In imitation of their Divine Model, many saints withdrew into the desert and lived in remote caves to escape the esteem of men. The desire to put ourselves forward and merit the plaudits of men, to be regarded as very successful in our undertakings, is, according to St. Vincent de Paul, an evil which causes us to forget our God; it vitiates our holiest actions and more than anything else impedes our progress in the spiritual life.

To be pleasing and acceptable in the sight of God, we must therefore banish from our hearts the desire to appear before men to win their approval and applause, and especially the desire to rule over others. "Inordinate ambition," writes Peter of Blois, "imitates charity but in a perverse manner. Charity endureth all things, but only for the sake of eternal goods; ambition endureth all things, but only for the wretched honors of this world. Charity is full of gentleness, especially towards the poor and despised; ambition is full of gentleness, but only towards the influential of this world who are in a position to satisfy its cravings. Charity believeth and hopeth all that pertains to eternal glory; ambition believes and hopes in everything that leads to the vain honor and glory of this world."

And granted that we attain the supposed honor for which we strive, what have we gained? What else but a little smoke that usually, instead of raising us, lowers us in the eyes of others. Honor vanishes, says St. Teresa, in consequence of the desire we have had to attain it. The greater the honor we receive, the greater the disgrace for having striven for it. St. Jane Chantal says: "The more worthy we think ourselves of some office or employment, the less worthy we are to have it, for we show that we are lacking in humility, which would be our best qualification." When St. Vincent Carafa of the Society of Jesus visited a sick friend who had just been appointed to a very important but dangerous office, the sick man begged him to pray for his recovery. St. Vincent replied: "No, my friend, I will not be unfaithful to my love for you. Now that you are in the state of grace, God calls you into the next world because He desires your salvation. Did He permit you to live, I know not whether you would save your soul in your new office." Hereupon the sick man quietly accepted death from the hand of God and died with perfect resignation.

TRUE DETACHMENT

Detachment from human beings does not mean that we are to love no one on this earth, but it means that our inclinations are to be in accordance with the Will of God and pleasing to Him. Both nature and religion impose upon us the obligation of loving our parents, relatives and benefactors. But this love becomes inordinate and bad when it leads us to offend God, and impedes our progress in a virtuous life. Many

Christians would make great progress on the road to perfection were they freed from all earthly attachments. But because they foster some inordinate attachment in their hearts and are unwilling to renounce it, they continue in their lamentable condition, without advancing a single step on the way of virtue. St. John of the Cross says: "A soul that is attached to any creature will never attain perfect union with God, even though that soul possess many other virtues." It matters very little whether a bird is bound with a strong or a weak cord, for the bird remains a captive and unable to fly as long as the cord is not broken. It is sad to see so many souls who are otherwise rich in virtues and graces, but who never reach a perfect union with God because they have not courage to renounce some little attachment. All that is necessary is one generous effort to break the cord that binds them and constitutes the only obstacle to their happiness.

To arrive at a perfect union with God, it is necessary, therefore, to be entirely detached from creatures. In particular we must renounce every inordinate attachment for our relatives. Our Lord and Saviour Jesus Christ tells us that he who is too much attached to relatives cannot be His disciple. And why? Because it often happens that we have no greater enemies of our soul than our own relatives. "A man's enemies are those of his household." (Matt. 10:36). St. Charles Borromeo said that as often as he visited his relatives, he returned with less zeal for the glory of God. When Father Antony Mendoza was asked why he never visited his parental home he replied: "Because I am aware that there is no place where religious so easily lose the spirit of piety as among their relatives."

He who has truly renounced inordinate attachment for his relatives will not be immoderately cast down when death claims someone who is near and dear to him. There are many who are inconsolable at the death of a relative or friend. They weep and moan and deliver themselves up to such unrestrained sadness and impatience that no one dares to approach them. I wonder whom they think they are pleasing by such unreasonable sadness and such a flood of tears! Is it God? Surely not; for God desires us to be resigned to His holy Will. Is it the soul of the deceased? Again, no; for if that soul is in Hell it spurns those tears and the one who sheds them. If it is saved and already in Heaven, then its greatest desire is that relatives and friends unite with it in thanking God. If the soul is still in Purgatory, it ardently longs for the prayers of its friends, and perfect resignation to God's Will so that all may be reunited one day in Heaven. To what purpose, therefore, such excessive weeping and lamentation? One day when the Venerable Theatine, Joseph Caracciolo, was visiting his relatives who constantly bemoaned the death of his brother, he said to them: "All, let us spare our tears for a more worthy object; let us shed them for the death of Jesus Christ, who is our Father, our Brother and our Spouse, and who suffered death for love of us." On such occasions we ought to imitate the pious Job, who on the death of his children said with beautiful resignation: "The Lord gave; the Lord hath taken away: as it hath pleased the Lord so is it done: blessed be the name of the Lord." (Job 1:21).

In the year 1624, the son of a pious Japanese was condemned to death. When the young man took leave of his mother, he spoke to her in the following words: "Dear mother, at last the hour is come for which I have yearned so long, and for which I have so often prayed to God. I am now going to die. Pardon me all the trouble and sorrow I have caused you, and give me a mother's blessing." He then knelt to receive her blessing. His mother embraced him tenderly and said: "My dear boy, may God bless you and grant you the grace to die a holy death. It pains my heart to lose you; but I am consoled with the thought that you die for

Jesus Christ. May He be forever blessed for this great grace He bestows on you." Hereupon the young man betook himself to the executioner to receive the stroke of death. What a magnificent example of detachment from relatives!

RESIGNATION TO GOD'S WILL

Detachment, moreover, requires us to be resigned to God's Will in the loss of those who are useful to us in our temporal or spiritual concerns. In this regard pious souls often commit serious faults by a want of resignation to the disposition of Divine Providence regarding their confessor. It is not confessors, but God, who makes us holy. When He gives them to us He desires us to profit by their sacred ministry in the affairs of our conscience; if He takes them from us, He wishes us to redouble our confidence in His goodness and to speak to Him in this manner: "Lord, Thou hast given me this assistance; now Thou takest it from me again; Thy holy will be done! Come Thou Thyself to my aid and teach me what I must do to be faithful to Thee!" Jesus Christ is our true Consolation, our true Leader, our true Love, yes, the only Love of our soul. He does not wish us to seek consolation outside Him. To be sure, God wills that we should not leave our spiritual director as long as we can have him; but when He Himself takes him away, He will give us another or supply his assistance in some other way.

Above all things, we must be detached from ourselves, that is, from our own will. He who knows how to overcome himself will easily conquer all other difficulties. It was this self-conquest that St. Francis Xavier so earnestly recommended to all who are striving after perfection. "If anyone will come after me," says our Blessed Lord, "let him deny himself." (Matt. 16:24). The epitome of all we must do to become holy is found in the single word, self-denial. We must therefore love God as God wishes and not as we desire. But God desires our soul to be empty of everything earthly in order to unite it to Himself and to fill it with His love. There are many who desire to attain to perfect union with God; but they are unwilling to bear the contradictions that God sends them. As long as they are not perfectly resigned to the Will of God, there is no thought of perfect union. "The way to union with God," says St. Catherine of Siena, "leads through afflictions and sorrows." These are the means God uses to purify us from all evil inclinations. Sickness, poverty, contempt, temptation and contradiction are permitted by God to give us an opportunity to battle against our inclinations and obtain the victory over our passions.

According to St. John of the Cross, "We must mortify our senses and desires." With regard to the senses we must, from love of Jesus Christ, reject every gratification that does not refer to the honor of God. For example, should a desire arise within us to see or hear things that are not calculated to bring us nearer to God, we must suppress such a desire. Moreover, our preference must be for the uncomfortable, the disagreeable and the bitter things that nature tries so hard to avoid. In one word, he who sincerely loves Jesus Christ will banish from his heart all attachment to earthly goods, and divest himself of everything in order to be perfectly united to his Blessed Redeemer. All his desires are centered in Jesus Christ. He is ever thinking of Him, ever yearning for Him. In every place and on all occasions he wishes to please Him alone. But to arrive at this sincere love it is necessary to banish from the heart all inclinations and attachments that are not for God.

What, therefore, must a soul do to give herself entirely to God? She must avoid whatever displeases God and do whatever is pleasing to Him. Secondly, she must accept whatever is sent her from the hand of God, however hard or disagreeable it may be. And thirdly, in all things she must prefer the Will of God to her own. In this manner we make a complete and worthy offering of the heart to God.

Chapter VI

Chastity

"Blessed are the clean of heart, for they shall see God."—Matt. 5:8

No one knows the value of chastity better than God Himself. Now God says: "No price is worthy of a continent soul." (Ecclus. 26:20). All that man prizes and esteems, riches, pleasures, honors, bear no comparison to a continent soul. St. Ephrem calls chastity "the life of the spirit." St. Peter Damian styles it "the queen of virtues," and St. Cyprian says by means of chastity we celebrate the most glorious triumphs. He who conquers the vice opposed to this virtue will easily triumph over the rest. On the contrary, he who permits himself to be ruled by incontinency falls an easy prey to the other vices such as hatred, injustice, etc. Chastity, says St. Ephrem, renders us in a certain sense like angels.

This comparison is altogether justified, for the life of angels is far from being a life of carnal gratifications. Angels are pure by nature; chaste souls are pure by reason of virtue. "On account of the merit of this virtue," says Cassian, "human beings are placed on a level with the angels." "Of course there is a difference," says St. Bernard, "between the chaste man and the angel, but it is not a difference of virtue; it is only one of happiness. If the chastity of the angels is more blessed, the chastity of man is more courageous."

St. Basil tells us that "chastity makes man very similar to God Himself, who is a pure spirit." On this account Our Lord chose a virgin for His Mother, a virgin for His foster father, St. Joseph, a virgin for His precursor, St. John the Baptist. St. Jerome says that Our Lord loved St. John the Apostle more than the rest on account of this virtue. To the virgin disciple He entrusted His Immaculate Mother, just as He now confides His Holy Church and His Sacred Presence in the Holy Eucharist to the care of the celibate priest. "O holy purity," says St. Athanasius, "thou art the dwelling place of the Holy Spirit, the life of angels and the crown of saints." How great, therefore, is the value of chastity! But how frightful the war that the flesh wages to rob us of this precious pearl!

Our body is the most powerful weapon the devil possesses to make us his slaves. On this account it is seldom that a man comes forth victorious from this conflict. "The struggle for chastity," says St. Augustine, "is the most violent of all; the battle is renewed every day, and victory is rare." "How many unfortunate persons there are," says St. Lawrence Justinian, "who having spent long years in solitude amid prayer, fasting and mortification, yielded at last to sensuality, gave up their holy life, and with the loss of chastity suffered the loss of God."

GREAT VIGILANCE NECESSARY

He, therefore, who would preserve the virtue of chastity must use the greatest precaution. "It is impossible for you to remain chaste," says St. Charles Borromeo, "unless you constantly watch over yourself. Negligence in this regard leads almost invariably to the loss of virtue." With regard to evil thoughts, there may be a twofold delusion. God-fearing souls who have little or no gift of discernment, and are inclined to scruples, think that every wicked thought that enters their mind is a sin. This is a mistake, for it is not the wicked thoughts in themselves that are sins, but the yielding or consenting to them. The wickedness of mortal sin consists in the perverse will which deliberately yields to sin with a complete knowledge of its wickedness and with full consent. And therefore St. Augustine teaches that when the consent of the will is absent, there is no sin. However much we may be tormented by temptations, the rebellion of the senses, or the inordinate motions of the inferior part of the soul, as long as there is no consent, there is no sin.

For the comfort of such anxious souls, let me suggest a good rule of conduct that is taught by all masters in the spiritual life. If a person who fears God and hates sin doubts whether he has consented to an evil thought or not, he is not bound to confess it, because it is morally certain that he has not given consent. For had he actually committed a mortal sin he would have no doubt about it, as mortal sin is such a monster in the eyes of one who fears God that its entrance into the heart could not take place without its being known.

Others, on the contrary, whose conscience is lax and not well-informed, think that evil thoughts and desires, though consented to, are not sins provided they are not followed by sinful actions. This error is worse than the one mentioned above. What we may not do, we may not desire. Therefore an evil thought or desire to which we consent comprises in itself all the wickedness of an evil deed. As sinful actions separate us from God, so wicked thoughts rob us of His grace. "Perverse thoughts separate us from God," says the Book of Wisdom (1:3).

From what has been said, it follows that not all evil thoughts are sinful and not all sinful thoughts are equal in malice. We must therefore distinguish between an evil thought that is a mortal sin, one that is venial, and one that is no sin at all. With regard to sins of thought, three things are to be taken into consideration: enticement, pleasure and consent. By enticement, or allurement, is meant the first thought that prompts us to commit the sin suggested to our senses. This enticement or suggestion is no sin; indeed, if it is rejected at once by the will it becomes a source of merit. "As often as you resist temptation," says St. Antoninus, "so often do you merit a crown." Even the Saints were tormented by such thoughts. To overcome a temptation of impurity St. Benedict rolled himself in a bed of thorns, and St. Peter of Alcantara plunged into the ice-cold water of a pond. St. Paul tells us he was tempted against holy purity! "And lest the greatness of the revelations should exalt me, there was given me a sting of my flesh, an angel of Satan to buffet me. For which thing thrice I besought the Lord, that it might depart from me. And he said to me: My grace is sufficient for thee: for power is made perfect in infirmity." (2 Cor. 12:7–9).

"When a thief is trying to break in a door," says St. Francis de Sales, "it is a sign he is not yet in the house. So, too, when the devil continues to tempt a soul it is a sign that soul is still in the grace of God." St. Catherine of Siena was once violently assaulted by the devil for the space of three days with temptations against holy purity. When Our Lord appeared to her to comfort her she cried out: "Ah my Saviour, where hast Thou been these three days?" Jesus answered: "I was in your heart, and it was I who gave you strength to resist those temptations." Our Lord then gave her to understand that her heart was purer after the assault than before.

Next to the enticement comes the pleasure. If the temptation is not rejected at once, a certain pleasure is experienced, and this it is that hurries one on to consent. As long as the will does not fully acquiesce, there is no mortal sin; at most it is venial. But if instant recourse is not had to God and every effort made to resist the temptation, the will is very apt to yield full consent and fall into grievous sin. A certain woman who was regarded as a saint was tempted one day by an evil thought. Failing to reject it at once, she became guilty of grievous sin. From false shame she neglected to confess the sinful thought she had yielded to, and shortly after, died. Now the Bishop of the place had considered her a saint, and accordingly he had her buried in his own chapel. On the following day the unfortunate soul appeared to him and declared that, owing to a sinful thought to which she had consented, she was eternally lost.

MEANS TO OVERCOME TEMPTATION

When assailed by such temptations, therefore, we must have instant recourse to the means necessary to overcome them. The first means consists in humbling oneself continually before God. David acknowledged that he had fallen into sin because he had not been humble and had trusted too much in himself. "Before I was humbled, I offended." (Ps. 118:67). Distrustful of self, therefore, we must place all our confidence in God. The second means is to have immediate recourse to God without stopping to consider the temptation. The best thing to do is to pronounce the holy names of Jesus and Mary and continue to pronounce them until the temptation is overcome. If it is a violent temptation it may be well to repeat the following resolution: "Oh my God, I will rather die than offend Thee! Oh my Jesus, help me! Mary, my Mother, assist me!" The names of Jesus and Mary have particular efficacy against the temptations of the devil.

The third means consists in often receiving the Sacraments of Penance and Holy Eucharist. It is of the greatest importance to reveal our temptations to our confessor. "A temptation revealed," says St. Philip Neri, "is half overcome." If one has the misfortune to yield to such temptations, no time should be lost in confessing it. As for Holy Communion, it is well to remember that this heavenly Food affords us great strength to resist temptations. The precious Blood of Jesus Christ which we receive in Holy Communion is called a "wine springing forth virgins." (Zach. 9:17). Earthly wine is a snare for chastity. This heavenly wine is its preservative.

A fourth means is devotion to the Immaculate Mother of God, the Virgin of virgins. Oh, how many have kept themselves pure as angels by devotion to this Blessed Queen of angels! Other means will suggest themselves to each individual, such as the avoidance of idleness, for "Idleness is the devil's workshop"; modesty of the eyes, and diligence in avoiding dangerous or proximate occasions. Nearly all the passions that assail us have their origin in the unrestrained liberty of the eyes, for as a rule it is our unguarded looks that awaken in us inordinate inclinations and passions. "I made a covenant with my eyes, that I would not so much as think upon a virgin," said Job (31:1). Why does he say: "so much as to think upon?" Should he not have said: "I have made a covenant not to look upon"? No, he was right in expressing himself as he did, for the thought and the look are so closely united as to be inseparable. In order, therefore, to have no evil thought, the holy man had resolved not to look at a virgin.

St. Augustine says: "From the look proceeds the thought and from the thought the desire." Had Eve not looked at the forbidden fruit, she would not have fallen into sin. But she took pleasure in looking at it, and the fruit seemed beautiful and good. She took it and ate and was guilty of disobedience. We see here how the devil tempts man first to look, then to desire, and at last to consent. Therefore, as St. Jerome says, the devil needs on our part only a beginning. It is enough if we only half open the door for him; he will then force it open all the way. A voluntary glance at a person of the opposite sex may be an infernal spark that will cause the ruin of the soul. "The first arrows that strike chaste souls," says St. Bernard, "and frequently cause deadly wounds, pierce through the eyes." It was the eyes that occasioned the fall of David, a man according to God's own heart. And so too with Solomon, who before had been the chosen instrument of the Holy Spirit. And many others have gone to destruction through their eyes. Seneca says that blindness is very useful for the preservation of innocence. In accordance with this principle, as Tertullian relates, a heathen philosopher deliberately deprived himself of sight in order to preserve chastity.

A Christian would not be permitted to do such a thing; but if we wish to preserve chastity, we must be blind insofar that we look at nothing which would awaken unclean thoughts within us. To this end we are exhorted by the Holy Ghost: "Gaze not upon another's beauty, for hereby lust is enkindled as a fire." (Ecclus. 9:8–9). The deliberate gaze is followed by sinful imaginations which enkindle the unholy fire. Therefore, St. Francis de Sales says: "He who does not wish the enemy to force his way into the fortress must keep the gates closed."

For this very reason the Saints have been exceedingly cautious about their eyes. For fear lest they should accidentally fall on some dangerous object they kept them nearly always cast down, and denied themselves the satisfaction of looking even at innocent objects. After St. Bernard had been a whole year in the novitiate, he did not know whether the ceiling of his cell was flat or arched. In the church of the monastery there were three windows; but St. Bernard did not know how many there were, for during that whole year he had not raised his eyes to gaze about. The holy Bishop Hugo never looked into the face of a woman with whom he happened to be speaking. St. Clare resolved never to look at the face of a man. One day when she raised her eyes to look at the Sacred Host she chanced to see the countenance of the priest, and she was very much disturbed.

When we consider these great precautions of the saints of God, how very imprudent and rash seems the conduct of those who, without the virtue of a St. Bernard or a St. Clare, gaze unconcernedly at persons of the opposite sex, and yet expect to remain free from temptations and the danger of sin. St. Jerome had retired into the grotto of Bethlehem, where he constantly prayed and mortified his body; and yet he was frightfully tormented by the recollection of those women whom he had seen long before at Rome. "What is injurious to us," says St. Francis de Sales, "is not so much the casual glance, but rather the intentional gaze." When Brother Roger, a Franciscan who was noted for his exceptional purity, was asked why he was so guarded in his looks, especially concerning women, he replied: "If man shuns the occasion, God protects him; if he deliberately puts himself in danger, the Lord abandons him and he easily falls into grievous sin."

If we suffer no other harm from the liberty we accord our eyes, we are at least deprived of recollection during prayer, because what we have seen will present itself again before the eyes of our soul and cause us endless distractions. Now, it is certain that a Christian who lives without interior recollection cannot practice the virtues, such as humility, patience, and mortification, in a proper manner. We must be careful, therefore, to direct our gaze to objects that will lead us to God and not from Him. "Downcast eyes," says St. Bernard, "direct the heart to Heaven." And St. Gregory Nazianzen writes: "'Where Christ dwells with His love, there recollection reigns."

A MEANS OF EDIFICATION

It is well to remember that the custody of the eyes is useful not only for our own sanctification, but also for the edification of others. God alone sees our heart; man sees only our external actions, and is either edified or scandalized by them. "A man is known by his look," says Holy Scripture (Ecclus. 19:26); that is to say, from the exterior we judge of the interior. Every Christian should therefore be what our Redeemer called St. John the Baptist: "a burning and a shining light." (John 5:35). Our interior should glow with divine love; our exterior should shine by Christian modesty. What St. Paul said to his disciples should apply also to us: "We are made a spectacle to the world, and to angels and to men." (1 Cor. 4:9). "Let your modesty be known to all men." (Phil. 4:5). It is related in the life of St. Francis of Assisi that one day he invited a religious brother to accompany him on a walk, saying he wished to preach. While going along he kept his eyes modestly cast down. After walking for a while he returned home. "When are you going to preach your sermon?" inquired his companion. "It is already preached," replied the Saint; "our sermon today consisted in mortifying our eyes, by which we edified all whom we met."

St. Ambrose says that the recollection of virtuous people is for the worldly-minded an excellent admonition. "What a beautiful thing it is," says the Saint, "that their mere appearance does good to others!" In this regard it is related of St. Bernardine of Siena that while still a young man in the world, his appearance was sufficient to restrain the unguarded remarks of his young companions. As soon as they saw him coming they would say to one another: "Be quiet; here comes Bernardine"; and they would either remain silent or begin some other topic of conversation. According to St. Gregory of Nyssa, St. Ephrem was so recollected that the very sight of him moved one to devotion, and one could not come in contact with him without feeling better for it.

More wonderful still is what Surius relates of the holy priest and martyr Lucian: "By his modesty and recollection alone he converted many heathens to the True Faith. The Emperor Maximian hearing this, and fearing that he too might be converted to Christianity, did not wish to look at him. When, therefore, he was summoned before the tribunal, the Emperor ordered him to stand behind a curtain so that he might talk to him without fear."

Our most perfect model in the practice of mortification of the eyes was our Divine Redeemer Himself. As a learned author remarks, the Evangelist expressly mentions that on certain occasions Jesus raised His eyes, indicating thereby that ordinarily He kept them cast down. Therefore the Apostle, when writing to his disciples, praises the modesty of his Divine Master: "I beseech you by the mildness and modesty of Christ." (2 Cor. 10:1).

Let us conclude these remarks with the words of St. Basil to his monks: "My dear sons, if we desire our soul to direct its gaze to Heaven, we must keep our eyes fixed on the earth. In the early morning as soon as we awake let us say with the royal Psalmist: 'Turn away my eyes that they may not behold vanity.'" (Ps. 118:37).

VIRGINITY

"They are the noblest portion of the Church of Christ," says St. Cyprian, when speaking of virgins who consecrate themselves to the love of their heavenly Spouse. Some of the holy Fathers, as St. Ephrem, St. Ambrose, and St. Chrysostom, have written whole books in praise of virginity. It is not my intention here to dwell at length on this beautiful subject, but merely to give a few ideas from which the devout reader may judge of its surpassing excellence.

In the first place, virginal souls are particularly dear in the sight of God. "They shall be as the angels of God in heaven," said our Blessed Redeemer. (Matt. 22:30).

Baronius relates that at the death of a virgin named Georgia, doves were seen flying about, and when her corpse was brought into the church they hovered over the spot where her remains were placed, nor did they leave until the virgin was buried. It was thought that these doves were angels who desired in this manner to show a last honor to her virginal body.

Virginal souls who consecrate themselves to the love of Jesus Christ become His chosen spouses. Wherefore St. Paul, when writing to his disciples, does not hesitate to say: "I have espoused you to Jesus Christ." In the parable of the virgins, Our Lord appears as the Bridegroom. By the faithful in general our Saviour is called Master, Shepherd, Father or Lord; by virginal souls He desires to be called Spouse. This espousal with the Divine Redeemer takes place through faith: "I will espouse thee to me in faith." (Osee 2:20). The virtue of virginity is, in an especial manner, the fruit of the merits of Jesus Christ; therefore we read in the Apocalypse that they "follow the Lamb whithersoever he goeth: These were purchased from among men, the first fruits to God and to the Lamb." (Apoc. 14:4).

The Divine Mother once revealed to a pious soul that those consecrated to Jesus Christ must, above all virtues, love holy purity, for it is this in particular that makes them similar to their heavenly Spouse. Prudent people of the world who desire to enter the state of matrimony are careful to inquire and find out who would most likely be the worthiest and most desirable partner for life. Those who enter the religious life are espoused to Christ by their holy vows. Let us turn, therefore, to the spouse in the Canticles to see what she has to say of the Divine Bridegroom. "My beloved is white and ruddy," she says (Cant. 5:10), white by reason of His purity, and ruddy on account of the glow of love with which He is inflamed towards His spouse. In a word, He is so beautiful, so perfect in every virtue, so kind and friendly that there is not and cannot be a nobler or more amiable spouse than He. St. Eucherius says: "There is nothing to compare with His majesty, His beauty, or His generosity."

A PRECIOUS TREASURE

St. Clare of Montefalco said that she prized her virginity so highly that she would rather suffer the torments of Hell during her whole lifetime than lose this precious treasure. Virtuous young women have even refused the proposal of marriage with kings in order to remain the spouses of Jesus Christ. Blessed Joanna,

Infanta of Portugal, rejected the hand of Louis XI, King of France. St. Agnes of Prague renounced a matrimonial alliance with the Emperor Frederick II; Elizabeth, the daughter of the King of Hungary and heiress to the throne, refused to be wedded to the Archduke of Austria. When Domitilla, the niece of the Emperor Domitian, was urged to marry the Count Aurelian, she replied: "If a person had the choice between a great monarch and a poor peasant, which would she choose as her bridegroom? Were I to marry Aurelian I would have to give up the King of Heaven; that would be the greatest folly, and I shall never be guilty of it." To her crown of virginity was added the crown of martyrdom, for her rejected lover had her burned to death.

A virgin who gives herself to the Lord, says Theodora, is freed from useless cares. She has nothing else to do but to deal confidently with the Lord. "Had she no other reward to expect," says St. Ambrose, "she would be happy indeed in being freed from worldly cares and anxieties and in occupying herself solely with God." But the peace and happiness she enjoys here on earth is but a foretaste of the great happiness and glory that await her in Heaven.

ACCEPTABLE TO GOD

Virgins who consecrate to God the lily of their chastity are as pleasing to Him as the holy angels. St. John was called the favorite Apostle of Our Lord, the Apostle whom Jesus loved, because he had preserved his virginity intact. For this very reason he was loved more than all the rest, and when our Saviour was dying on the Cross He committed His Immaculate Mother to the care of His virgin disciple, St. John. The great value of virginity is enhanced in our eyes by the extraordinary praise which the Holy Ghost bestows upon it: "No price is worthy of a continent soul." (Ecclus. 26:20). The Blessed Virgin Mary taught us this when the Archangel Gabriel brought her the message from on high: that God wished to become man and to choose her for His Mother. To the angel's words Mary humbly replied: "How can this be, for I know not man?" (Luke 1:34). By these words our Blessed Lady showed that she preferred to renounce the dignity of the Mother of God than to lose the treasure of her virginity. According to St. Cyprian, virginal purity is the queen of all virtues and the perfection of all goods. They who preserve their purity for the love of Jesus Christ, says St. Ephrem, are particularly favored by Him. St. Bernardine adds that virginity disposes the soul in an especial manner to see God by faith in this life and by the light of eternal glory in the next. One day God showed His great servant, Lucretia Orsini, the throne of glory prepared for those who serve Jesus Christ in virginal purity. Ravished in ecstasy, the Saint exclaimed: "Oh how dear to God and His holy Mother are virginal souls!"

"My son, when thou comest to the service of the Lord prepare thy soul for temptation." (Ecclus. 2:1). Be prepared therefore to suffer with humility and patience, for "silver and gold are tried by fire." No man can serve two masters, God and the world. He, therefore, who desires to consecrate himself to God, must renounce the world and say with all sincerity: God alone is my treasure and my only good. A heart that truly loves God despises the world and all that the world can offer; in a word, it despises all that is not God.

The venerable Francisca Farnese knew no more effectual means of exhorting her religious Sisters to the practice of perfection than to remind them that they were the spouses of Jesus Christ. "It is certain," she would say, "that each one of you is chosen by God to become a saint, since He has given you the great honor of being His spouse." And in very truth this is an inestimable grace which deserves our most generous cooperation. St. Augustine, when writing to a virgin consecrated to God, made use of these words: "You must know that you have a Spouse who is more beautiful than anything that earth or Heaven contains, and in choosing you to be His bride He has given you a most certain pledge of His love. From this you will recognize your obligation to love Him in return."

Should the world attempt to win your love, O spouse of Jesus Christ, answer in the words of the noble St. Agnes: "Away, away; you seek my love, but I can love none other than my God who has loved me first." "As you are the spouse of a God," says St. Jerome, "you should be proud of such a distinction." People of the world feel highly honored and make much ado about matrimonial alliances with the noble and wealthy. You have something more than this to be proud of, since you are affianced to the King of Heaven Himself. You can well say with a holy pride and joy: "I have found Him whom my soul loveth; I will embrace Him with my love, and I will never leave Him."

Love is the bond which unites the soul to God. Say often in the words of the Apostle St. Paul: "Who shall separate me from the love of Christ? Shall tribulation, or distress or famine, or nakedness, or danger or persecution or the sword? . . . I am sure that neither death nor life, nor angels, nor principalities, nor powers, nor things present nor things to come, nor might, nor height, nor depth nor any other creature shall be able to separate me from the love of God which is in Christ Jesus Our Lord." (Rom. 8:38–39).

Chapter VII

Obedience

"You are my friends, if you do the things that I command you."—John 15:14

Perfection consists in the conformity of our will to the Will of God. Now what is the surest means of knowing God's Will, and of regulating our lives according to it? It is obedience towards our lawful superiors. "Never is the Will of God more perfectly fulfilled," says St. Vincent de Paul, "than when we obey our superiors."

The greatest sacrifice that a soul can make to God consists in obedience to lawfully constituted superiors; for as, in the opinion of St. Thomas, "nothing is dearer to us than the liberty of our will," we can offer to God no more acceptable gift than this very liberty. "Obedience is better than sacrifices," says the Holy Ghost (1 Kings 15:22); that is to say, God prefers obedience to all other sacrifices. He who gives his property to God, by distributing it among the poor; his honor, by patiently bearing contempt; his body, by fasts and penitential works, gives Him a part of himself. But he who offers God his will, by subjecting it to obedience, gives Him all he has, and can truly say: "My Lord, after I have given Thee my will, I have nothing more to give." As St. Gregory says: "By the other virtues we give to God what belongs to us; by obedience we give Him ourselves." The same Saint teaches that all the other virtues follow in the train of obedience and by its influence are preserved in the soul.

A GREAT REWARD

According to the Venerable Sertorius Caputo, the reward of obedience is similar to that of martyrdom. In martyrdom we offer to God the head of our body; by obedience we offer Him our will, which is the head of the soul. Therefore the Wise Man assures us that "an obedient man shall speak of victory." (Prov. 21:28). It is easy, says St. Gregory, for those who obey, to overcome all the attacks of Hell; for, since by obedience they subject their will to men, they rise superior to the demons who fell on account of their disobedience. Cassian adds that if we mortify our self-will, we can easily root out all vices, because the latter spring from the former.

St. Augustine says that while Adam through disobedience brought destruction upon himself and all his posterity, the Son of God became man to redeem us and to teach us true wisdom by His life of obedience. For this reason He began as a child to practice obedience when He was subject to Mary and Joseph: "He was subject to them," says St. Luke (2:51). What our Saviour began as a child He continued His whole life, so that St. Paul could say: "He was obedient unto death, even to the death of the cross." (Phil. 2:8). The Mother of God revealed to one of her servants that Our Lord when dying for us entertained a very special love for obedient souls. To increase our merit, Our Lord desires us to be guided by faith. Therefore, instead of speaking to us Himself, He makes His Will known to us by means of our superiors.

When Jesus appeared to St. Paul and converted him on the road to Damascus, the future Apostle said: "Lord, what wilt Thou have me to do?" The Lord could easily have instructed him then and there, but He did not; He merely said: "Arise and go into the city, and there it shall be told thee what thou must do." (Acts 9:7). Accordingly, St. Giles maintains that we gain more merit by obeying man for the love of God than by obeying God Himself. When we obey lawful superiors we are more sure of doing the Will of God than if Jesus Christ Himself would appear and speak to us. Such an apparition might afford us no certainty that it really was our Saviour who appeared and spoke; the evil spirit can appear as an angel of light in order to deceive us. But when we receive a command from our superiors, we are certain that in obeying them we are obeying Jesus Christ Himself. "He that heareth you, heareth me." (Luke 10:16).

A SOURCE OF MERIT

It is a delusion, therefore, to imagine that we can do anything better than that which is prescribed by obedience. To leave the occupation we are in duty bound to perform, in order to be united with God in meditation or spiritual reading is rather, according to St. Francis de Sales, to leave God in order to follow more closely the dictates of our self-love. From a soul that is resolved to serve God, says St. Teresa, God desires but one thing, and that one thing is obedience. "What we do from obedience," says Rodriguez, "is of more value than any other work we can perform."

It is more meritorious to pick up a straw from the ground, out of obedience, than from self-will to make a long meditation or scourge ourselves to blood. St. Mary Magdalen de Pazzi preferred an exercise prescribed by obedience even to prayer. "When I am acting out of obedience," she said, "I am certain that I am doing the Will of God, but at other times this is not the case." All the masters of the spiritual life are unanimous in asserting that it is better to omit a pious exercise from obedience than to perform it against obedience. The Blessed Virgin revealed to St. Bridget that he who from obedience omits an act of mortification gains a double merit: that of the mortification he would like to perform, and that of obedience for the sake of which he omits it. St. Teresa was therefore right in saying that obedience is the shortest way to perfection. Christian soul, if you desire to walk securely, be guided in all your actions by obedience. Merchants and business men have their property insured in order not to suffer loss from its destruction. In order to render safe your eternal reward, make sure to get the security of obedience for all your actions.

QUALITIES OF OBEDIENCE

Obedience, however, to have this high value must be supernatural. To obey the Church, our parents, our confessor, in a word, our spiritual and temporal superiors in a meritorious way, we must be persuaded that obedience towards our superiors is obedience shown to God, and contempt for their commands is contempt shown to our Divine Master Himself, for He has said to our superiors: "He that heareth you heareth me, and he that despiseth you despiseth me." (Luke 10:16). The Apostle St. Paul, writing to his disciples, says: "Obey, not serving to the eye, as it were pleasing men, but as the servants of Christ, doing the will of God from the heart." (Eph. 6:6).

If, then, an order is given you by your parents, your confessor or your superiors, you must execute it not merely to please them, but principally to please God, whose will is made known to you by your superiors. By so doing you are more certain of fulfilling the Will of God than if an angel came down from Heaven and revealed it to you. St. Paul, when writing to the Galatians, says: "If an angel from Heaven preach a gospel to you besides that which we have preached to you, let him be anathema." (Gal. 1:8). Keep this truth constantly before your eyes: when you obey your superiors you are obeying God. If Our Lord came in person and charged you with some office or some particular work, would you hesitate a moment to obey? Would you begin to excuse yourself and oppose obstacles to the fulfillment of His command? But, says St. Bernard, whether it is God Himself or one who takes His place that gives the command, you must render the same prompt and cheerful obedience.

OBEDIENCE TO PARENTS

With regard to the obedience due to parents, St. Paul says: "Children, obey your parents in the Lord, for this is just." (Eph. 6:1). It must here be observed that the Apostle says, "obey your parents in the Lord," that is to say, in those things that are pleasing to the Lord, but not in those that displease Him. If, for example, a mother were to command her son to steal, or to injure another, would he be obliged to obey? Certainly not; were he to obey in such a case he would be guilty of sin. Again, St. Thomas teaches that children are not obliged to obey their parents when there is question of the choice of a state of life. With reference to the married state, Pinamonti with Sanchez, Konink and others, maintains that young people are obliged to consult their parents, since they are more experienced, and may often prevent serious mistakes. Moreover, to ignore them in a matter which they have so much at heart is most certain to wound them keenly. But with regard to vocation to the religious life, a child is not in the least bound to ask his parents' advice, because in this matter they have no experience and their prejudices generally make them hostile. Parents who unreasonably prevent their children from following a vocation to the priesthood or the religious life are guilty of unspeakable cruelty towards their own offspring. "A man's enemies shall be they of his own household." (Matt. 10:36).

The condition of servants is lowly and contemptible in the eyes of the world, but not so to the eyes of faith. This we learn from the example of our Blessed Redeemer Himself, who, though Lord of Heaven and earth, "emptied himself, taking the form of a servant, being made in the likeness of men, and in habit found as a man." (Phil. 2:7). He humbly obeyed His Blessed Mother and St. Joseph, eminently holy creatures it is true, but infinitely below Him in dignity: "He was subject to them." (Luke 2:51). When instructing His Apostles He said: "He that will be first among you let him be your servant. Even as the Son of man is not come to be ministered unto, but to minister." (Matt. 20:28).

It is hardly necessary to say that servants are not bound to obey when they are commanded to do what God forbids. When the tyrant Antiochus wished to force the old man Eleazar to disregard the law which interdicted the use of pork to the Hebrews, the friends of the aged Eleazar took pity on him and suggested that he might escape death by pretending to eat of the forbidden food. But Eleazar replied: "It doth not become our age to dissemble: whereby many young persons might think that Eleazar, at the age of fourscore and ten years, was gone over to the life of the heathens; and so they, through my dissimulation, and for a little time of a corruptible life, should be deceived, and hereby I should bring a stain and a curse upon my old age. For though at the present time I should be delivered from the punishments of men, yet should I not escape the hand of the Almighty neither alive nor dead. Wherefore by departing manfully out of this life I shall show myself worthy of my old age, and I shall leave an example of fortitude to young men, if with a ready mind and constancy I suffer an honorable death, for the most venerable and most holy laws." (2 Mach. 6:24–28).

OBEDIENCE TO OUR SPIRITUAL DIRECTOR

Obedience to our spiritual director is of the greatest importance if we desire to please God and make progress in perfection. "It is true," says St. Gregory, "that some saints have been guided directly by God"; "but," he continues, "such examples are rather to be admired than imitated, for, thinking ourselves above the guidance of men, we might easily be led into error." Virtue is found in the golden mean; as idleness in the spiritual life is a fault, so too is intemperate zeal. It is the duty of the spiritual director to war against the former and to moderate the latter. Almighty God could direct us very well without the aid of another, but to keep us humble He desires us to submit to the authority and guidance of His servants.

Our Lord has indeed bestowed a great benefit on us in giving us spiritual guides to prevent us from going astray. Many people think that sanctity consists in performing works of penance. But if a person of weak constitution were to perform works of penance, and thereby seriously endanger his life, would he be laboring at his sanctification? Assuredly not; he would rather be guilty of sin. Others imagine that sanctity consists in much praying. But if the father of a family neglected the care of his children in order to go into solitude and pray, he would be guilty of sin. Still others imagine that sanctity consists in the frequent reception of Holy Communion. But suppose that the mother of a family would neglect her household duties and inconvenience her husband and her children for the sake of going to Holy Communion every day—she would have to give an account of her conduct to God.

In what, then, does sanctity consist? It consists in the perfect fulfillment of God's Will. But how shall we know what God desires of us? Thank God that He has given us a means of knowing. He tells us that by obeying our spiritual director we are obeying Him: "He that heareth you, heareth me." St. Teresa says: "We must make our confessor our judge and then be at rest with regard to the affairs of our soul, placing all our confidence in the words of Our Lord: 'He that heareth you, heareth me.'" This is the surest way, she says, of fulfilling the Will of God. The Saint tells us that she herself, by obedience to her confessor, learned to know and love God.

Speaking on this subject, St. Francis de Sales said: "We find the most important of all admonitions in the words of the devout Avila: 'You may seek where you will, nowhere will you so surely find the Will of God as on the road of this humble obedience which all the Saints have recommended and practiced.'"

Obedience to our spiritual director is very pleasing to God, whether it is exercised in praying, in receiving Holy Communion, in mortifying ourselves or in omitting these holy exercises. We are always gaining merit, whether we eat or drink or recreate ourselves; for while we are obeying our confessor we are doing the Will of God. Holy Scripture says that obedience is more pleasing to God than all the other sacrifices we could make. Obey your spiritual Father, says St. Paul (Heb. 13:17), and be without fear regarding what you do out of obedience, for it is not you but he that will have to render an account of your actions. St. Philip Neri says: Those who desire to make progress in the way to perfection must choose a well-informed confessor and obey him as they would God Himself. Whoever does this is sure to have no account to give before God of what he has done or left undone. If, therefore, on judgment day Jesus Christ were to ask you: Why have you chosen this state of life? Why have you omitted this or that act of mortification? You can, provided you have practiced obedience, reply in these words: Lord, my confessor ordered me to do so—and then the Divine Judge must needs sanction what you have done.

On the other hand, if we refuse to obey the voice of our spiritual director we run the risk of being eternally lost. "He that heareth you, heareth me; and he that despiseth you, despiseth me." (Luke 10:16). God said the same thing to Samuel when he complained that the people whom the Lord had entrusted to his care, had despised him: "They have not rejected thee, but me." (1 Kings 8:7). As a ship that is abandoned by its pilot, or a patient that is forsaken by his physician, so is the soul that is deprived of the guidance of a spiritual director.

We must be convinced, however, that no spiritual director can lead us to sanctity unless we are determined to renounce our own will. And as for peace of heart, remember well it is to be looked for not from the confessor, but from God Himself.

THE VOW OF OBEDIENCE

St. Thomas teaches that it is the vow of obedience that makes the religious. On this account St. Teresa used to say that a religious who is not obedient is not deserving of the name of religious. On the other hand, a religious who practices obedience is on the shortest road to perfection. "O virtue of obedience," she cries out, "thou dost accomplish everything!" St. Catherine of Bologna said that obedience alone is more pleasing to God than all other good works. When the Venerable Leonardi, Founder of the Clerics Regular of the Mother of God, was asked by his disciples to give them a Rule, he wrote on a sheet of paper just this one word: "Obedience." By this he wished to show, as Sertorious Caputo remarks, that in religious life obedience and sanctity are one and the same thing. Thoroughly convinced of this truth, St. Anselm on becoming Archbishop of Canterbury and finding no one above him, induced the Holy Father to make his chaplain his superior, whom he obeyed in everything. According to the opinion of St. Bonaventure, all the perfection of the religious life consists in the renunciation of self-will. Obedience to the rules and the commands of superiors is the greatest sacrifice a soul can make to God. It is certain that a religious who obeys exactly acquires rich treasures of merit.

St. Aloysius Gonzaga compared the religious life to a sailboat on which a person can make progress without the use of oars. And it is very true, for in religious life not only when we fast, or pray, or meditate, but also when we take our meals, our rest or recreation, we are acquiring merit; for as all this is done out of obedience, the Will of God is accomplished and merit is thereby gained. In the life of the ancient Fathers it is related that one of them saw two choirs of the blessed in Heaven; one of the choirs consisted of those who had left the world and had lived in solitude, devoted to a life of prayer and penance; the other choir was made up of those who had subjected themselves to a life of obedience for the love of Jesus Christ and had lived entirely according to the will of their superiors. These latter enjoyed a greater degree of glory than the former; for though the hermits had pleased God by their spiritual exercises, they nevertheless had done their own will, whereas the others, by means of the vow of obedience had given their will to God, the best offering they could make Him.

St. Dorotheus relates something similar in reference to his disciple St. Dositheus. The latter had very poor health, and in consequence was unable to perform the customary exercises with the rest of the community; in order not to lose any merit thereby, he made a perfect renunciation of his will and devoted himself entirely to the practice of obedience. After five years he departed this life. Now, God revealed to the Abbot Dorotheus that this holy youth had obtained in Heaven a reward equal to that of the holy hermits, St. Paul and

St. Antony. The monks were surprised that Dositheus should have attained such great glory, as he had not even done as much as the others; but God made known to them that it was due to his obedience that Dositheus had been so richly rewarded.

If you ask me what is the best and most effectual means of obeying in a meritorious manner, I answer: "Be thoroughly persuaded that when you are obeying your superior, you are obeying God, and when you despise the command of your superior you are despising the Divine Redeemer Himself." St. John Climacus relates that the superior of a cloister once called an old monk, and, to give the others an example, he bade him remain standing for a long time. When later they asked the old monk what were his sentiments during this mortification, he replied: "I imagined that I stood before Jesus Christ, and that He Himself had imposed upon me this humiliation, and therefore I had not the slightest thought against obedience."

OBSERVANCE OF THE RULE

To St. Francis de Sales are attributed these very significant words: "The predestination of religious is bound up with the observance of their rule." St. Mary

Magdalen de Pazzi was accustomed to say that obedience to the rule is the shortest and surest way to sanctity and eternal happiness. Indeed for religious, the observance of the rule is the only means of becoming holy; no other way leads to this coveted goal. A religious who would habitually violate the rules of the institute would not advance a single step in the love of Jesus Christ, even though he performed works of penance and were devoted to spiritual exercises. The efforts of such religious are all in vain and in them are fulfilled the words of the Holy Ghost: "He that rejecteth wisdom and discipline is unhappy; and their hope is vain, and their labors without fruit and their works unprofitable." (Wis. 3:11).

The rules of a religious are, no doubt, a burden, but a burden like that of wings, by means of which we are borne aloft to God. "The burden of Jesus Christ," says St. Augustine, "has wings that enable us to rise above the earth." The rules of a religious are bonds, but bonds of love that unite us to the highest and greatest good. If it seems hard to us that the rule forbids what self-love demands, let us say joyfully with the Apostle: "I am a prisoner of the Lord" (Eph. 4:1), but I rejoice in my bonds because they unite me more closely to my God and secure for me an eternal crown.

It may be that you can do nothing great for the Lord; you are unable to perform severe penances or to spend much time at prayer. You can at least be exact in the observance of the rule, and this alone is sufficient in a short time to further your progress in perfection. St. Bonaventure says: "The best way to strive after perfection is to observe everything that is prescribed." The measure of our generosity in this regard will be the measure of God's bounty toward us. St. Augustine called the rules the mirror of religious because from our zeal in observing them we can know what we look like in the eyes of God. "It is better," says a learned author, "to be a finger united to the body than an eye separated from it." An apparently good work, but one not in accordance with the rule, is not acceptable to God, and is only an obstacle to our striving after perfection. In the eyes of the world many of the rules of religious life are insignificant trifles, but they are not so when considered in the light of faith. When Michael Angelo was asked why he paid so much attention to trifles, he said: "Trifles go to make up perfection, and perfection is no trifle." St. Giles once said: "By a little negligence we may lose a great grace."

In order to observe the rules perfectly, says St. Ignatius, love must be our motive, not fear; in other words, we must observe our rules not merely to avoid the reproofs of our superiors or to be praised by others, but simply and solely for the love of Jesus Christ. To be perfect, says Father Pavone of the Society of Jesus, obedience must walk on both feet. By this he meant that perfect obedience includes both the will and the intellect. St. Mary Magdalen de Pazzi expressed a similar sentiment when she said: "Perfect obedience requires a soul without a will, and a will without a judgment." One day St. Ignatius remarked that if the Pope were to command him to make a voyage on the high sea in a little boat without rudder or sail, he would blindly obey. When someone objected that it would be very imprudent to put himself in such danger of death, the Saint replied: "Prudence is required of superiors; the prudence of subjects must consist in obeying without prudence."

The great St. Bernard said: "If, instead of obeying blindly, we wish to know why the superior has ordered this or that, we show that our obedience is very imperfect." It was in this way that the devil tempted Eve and brought about her fall. "Why," said he, "has God forbidden you to eat of all the trees in the garden?" Eve would not have fallen into sin had she answered: "It is not for us to inquire into the reason of this prohibition;

we have only to obey." But unfortunately, she began to wonder why it was that such a command had been given, and replied: "Lest perhaps we should die." From that one word "perhaps" the devil perceived that she had begun to waver, and at once he said: "Do not fear; you will not die." And Eve fell, and misfortune came upon the whole human race.

Chapter VIII

Meekness and Humility

"Learn of me, because I am meek and humble of heart."—Matt. 11:29

Humility is called by the saints the foundation and safeguard of all the virtues. If it is not the most prominent among the virtues, it occupies, according to St. Thomas, the first place as the foundation of the rest. In the erection of a building, the basement comes before the walls and pillars, even though the latter be of gold. And so in the spiritual life humility must precede everything else in order to banish pride, to which God is so opposed. He, therefore, who endeavors to acquire the other virtues without humility, says St. Gregory, is scattering dust before the wind.

The virtue of humility was little known and less loved on earth; indeed, it was thoroughly despised.

Pride reigned everywhere, for it was an unfortunate inheritance of the human race bequeathed to his posterity by Adam. The Son of God descended from Heaven to teach man by word and example the value of humility, and with this end in view He went so far as to "empty himself, taking the form of a servant, being made in the likeness of men, and in habit found as a man. He humbled himself . . . even to the death of the cross." (Phil. 2:7). His first appearance on earth was in the humble stable of Bethlehem; the greater portion of His mortal life was spent in humble retirement at Nazareth. He departed this life, humbled and despised, on the summit of Mt. Calvary; and He calls out to each one of us: "I have given you an example that as I have done, so you do also." (John 13:15). By this He means to say: "My dear children, I have endured all this humiliation and contempt that you might follow My example." With regard to the humility of Jesus Christ, St. Augustine says: "If this medicine does not cure us of pride, I know not what other remedy can do so."

PRIDE AN ABOMINATION TO THE LORD

"Every proud man is an abomination to the Lord," says the Holy Ghost. (Prov. 16:5). The proud man is a thief because he appropriates what belongs to God from whom, as St. Paul says, he has received everything.

If a horse were decked with gorgeous trappings would it—supposing it were able to do so—pride itself on having such fine adornments, knowing that at a moment's notice its master could take them away? The proud man is guilty of falsehood, for all the goods that he possesses both in the order of nature and grace are the gifts of God. "By the grace of God I am what I am," says the Apostle (1 Cor. 15:10), for "we are not sufficient to think any thing of ourselves, as of ourselves, but our sufficiency is from God." (2 Cor. 3:5).

"Humble yourself," says St. Augustine, "and God will descend to unite Himself with you; but if you are proud He will depart from you." The Royal Prophet had said the same thing long before: God looks upon the humble with loving eyes, but the proud He sees from afar. When the rebel angels grew proud, God drove them from His sight and cast them into the abyss, for God's Word must be fulfilled: "Whosoever shall exalt himself, shall be humbled." (Matt. 23:12). St. Peter Damian relates that a certain proud man once heard these words of Our Lord read in the Gospel at Holy Mass. "That is not true," he said, "for if I humbled myself I would lose my possessions and the respect of my fellowmen." Now what happened? He fought a duel in defense of his property, and his antagonist, striking him in the mouth with his weapon, pierced his blasphemous tongue and stretched him dead on the ground.

The Lord has promised to hear all who call upon Him: "Everyone that asketh, receiveth." (Matt. 7:8). But to the proud man God will not listen. "God resisteth the proud," says St. James, "and giveth grace to the humble." (Jas. 4:6). Yes, God hastens to open His hand and bestow upon the humble what they desire. "Lord, give me the treasure of humility," prayed St. Augustine. Humility is called a treasure because the Lord sees to it that the humble abound in good things. When man's heart is full of himself, there is no room for God's gifts. Man must therefore, as it were, be emptied of himself by the knowledge of his own nothingness. "He that is mighty hath done great things to me" said the Blessed Virgin Mary, "because he hath regarded the humility of his handmaid" (Luke 1:48);

that is to say, He hath considered the knowledge I have of my own nothingness.

A SOURCE OF BLESSINGS

St. Teresa tells us that she received the greatest graces from God when she humbled herself most profoundly in His presence. "The prayer of him that humbleth himself shall pierce the clouds; and he will not depart till the most High behold." (Ecclus. 35:21). St. Joseph Calasanctius used to say: "If you desire to be holy, be humble; if you desire to be very holy, be very humble." This advice was given by a devout man to St. Francis Borgia before he had entered the religious life: "If you want to become a saint, think of your own misery and wretchedness." Following this advice, the Saint spent two hours every day trying to obtain a knowledge and contempt of himself. "As pride," says St. Gregory, "is the most evident characteristic of the reprobate, humility is the clearest sign of the elect." When St. Anthony, the hermit, saw the world full of the snares of the devil, he cried out: "Who can ever escape so many dangers?" He heard a voice say: "Anthony, humility alone walks securely; he who goes with head bowed down, need not fear to fall into these snares." In a word, if we do not become children—not of course in age, but in humility—we cannot, as our Saviour said, enter the Kingdom of Heaven. "Learn of me, for I am meek, and humble of heart: and you shall find rest to your souls." (Matt. 11:29).

The proud man has no peace or rest, for he is seldom, if ever, treated in a manner corresponding to the exalted opinion he has of himself. If he is honored, he is dissatisfied that others are honored more than he. There is always a little more honor that he might have had, the absence of which annoys him more than what he has affords him pleasure. What great honor, for example, did not Aman enjoy at the court of Assuerus? It was his privilege to eat at the king's table, and yet he was unhappy because Mardochai would not salute him. "And whereas I have all these things, I think I have nothing, so long as I see Mardochai sitting before the King's gate." (Esther 5:13). St. Jerome says that true honor avoids him who seeks it and seeks him who avoids it; it is like a shadow that follows the one who flees from it and flees from the one who follows it.

The humble man, on the contrary, is always content. If honor is shown to him, he regards it as above his deserts; if he is offended, he considers himself as deserving of worse treatment than he has received, and he says with Job: "I have sinned and indeed I have offended, and I have not received what I have deserved." (Job 33:27).

On one occasion when St. Francis Borgia was travelling, he was advised to send someone ahead to secure a lodging and prevent the inconveniences attending an unexpected arrival. The Saint replied: "As far as that is concerned, I always send a quartermaster ahead. My quartermaster is the thought of the Hell that I have deserved. As a result, every lodging is like a king's palace for me compared to the place where I deserve to be."

HUMILITY OF INTELLECT

The virtue of humility is twofold, namely, humility of the intellect and humility of the will. According to St. Bernard, humility of the intellect consists in having an humble opinion of ourselves and in regarding ourselves as deserving of contempt. Humility is truth, writes St. Teresa, and therefore the Lord loves the humble so much because He loves the truth. It is certainly true that of ourselves we are nothing; we are ignorant and blind and incapable of accomplishing any good. On the one hand, we have nothing of our own but sin, which makes us still more contemptible. On the other hand, of ourselves we can do nothing but commit sin. Everything good that we may have or can do, comes from God and belongs to God. Now the humble man has this truth ever before his eyes, and consequently he ascribes nothing to himself but sin, which makes him deserving of contempt. He cannot bear to have merit ascribed to him that he does not deserve, but he rejoices in his soul when he is called upon to suffer contempt.

We must therefore say with the great St. Augustine: "Grant, O Lord, that I may know who I am and who Thou art." Thou art the source of all good and I am nothing but misery and wretchedness. "Only by the humble," says the Wise Man, "is God truly honored." (Ecclus. 3:21). If you wish therefore to honor God, humbly acknowledge your own wretchedness and protest your willingness to receive whatever treatment God's providence has in store for you. Never boast of your good works. Read the lives of the Saints to see what they have done, and then feel ashamed of yourself for having accomplished so little. The Venerable John of Avila relates that a celebrated man who had married a peasant girl insisted that she should not destroy her poor clothes, but keep them so that she might not grow proud when she saw herself surrounded by servants and clad in costly attire. We must act in a similar manner. When we perceive anything good in ourselves, we must look at our old clothes. In other words we must recall to mind what we once were, and draw the conclusion that everything good that we possess is an alms bestowed by God. Whenever St. Teresa performed a good work or saw one performed, she hastened to thank God for it.

In the next place, we must try to realize that without God's assistance we can do nothing, absolutely nothing. This will lead us to distrust ourselves and place implicit confidence in God. St. Peter trusted in his own strength when he said: "Even though I should die with thee, I will not deny thee." (Matt. 26:35). But we know how soon after he not only denied, but protested under oath that he did not know Our Lord. Put your confidence in God and say with St. Paul: "I can do all things in him who strengtheneth me." (Phil. 4:13). When St. Catherine of Siena was tempted she humbled herself and put all her confidence in God. One day the devil cried out in a rage: "Cursed be thou, and cursed be he who taught thee this means of overcoming me."

HUMILITY OF WILL

Humility of the intellect, as we have seen, consists in acknowledging that we are nothing and deserving only of contempt. Humility of the will consists in the desire to be despised by others and in the pleasure such contempt affords us. Humility of the will Our Lord had especially in view when He said: "Learn of me, because I am meek, and humble of heart." (Matt. 11:29). Many are humble with their lips but not in their heart. They acknowledge that they are wicked and deserving of punishment, but when they are reproved they deny that they are at fault. "To humble oneself for the sake of being praised," says St. Bernard, "is not humility at all; in fact it is destructive of humility, for by such conduct humility itself becomes an object of pride." "He," says St. Joseph Calasanctius, "who loves God, does not wish to appear holy, but desires to be so." The saints have not become saints in the midst of approval and applause; it was rather amid insults and contempt. The holy martyr Ignatius, when Bishop, enjoyed universal esteem and reverence; he was afterwards dragged to Rome, as a criminal, to be cast to the wild beasts. On the journey thither the guards loaded him with insults and outrages of all kinds. The Saint cried out with joy: "Now I begin to be a disciple of Christ."

He who knows not how to bear an insult shows plainly that he has lost sight of Jesus Crucified. The Venerable Mary of the Incarnation said to her sister religious one day at the sight of the crucifix: "Is it possible, dear Sisters, that we can refuse to suffer contempt when we see Jesus Christ so despised?" Our Saviour once appeared to St. John with a cross on His shoulder and a crown of thorns encircling His head. "John," said He, "ask of me what you wish." The Saint replied: "Lord, I desire to suffer and to be despised for Thee."

A very devout person had the beautiful custom of going before the Blessed Sacrament whenever she was insulted or offended. Kneeling before the tabernacle, she would say: "O my God, I am too poor to offer Thee anything precious or costly; therefore I offer Thee this little gift that I have just received." If, therefore, Christian soul, you desire to attain great sanctity, you must be prepared to suffer humiliation and contempt. Does this seem hard for poor human nature? Then remember the promise of our Saviour Jesus Christ: "Blessed are ye when men shall revile you, and persecute you, and speak all that is evil against you, untruly, for my sake: Be glad and rejoice, for your reward is very great in heaven." (Matt. 5:11).

MEEKNESS

Humility and meekness were the favorite virtues of Jesus Christ, and He recommended them in a particular manner to His disciples when He said: "Learn of me, because I am meek, and humble of heart." (Matt. 11:29). Our Divine Redeemer was called the "Lamb of God," not only on account of the Sacrifice He was to make of Himself on the Cross in expiation for sin, but also on account of the meekness that characterized His whole life and particularly during His bitter Passion. When He was rudely buffeted by the servant of Caiphas and charged with a want of respect for the high priest, He meekly replied: "If I have spoken ill, give testimony thereof; but if well, why strikest thou me?" (John 18:23). When He hung upon the Cross and His enemies loaded Him with insults and ignominy, He turned to His heavenly Father and said: "Father, forgive them, for they know not what they do." (Luke 23:34).

How dear to God are those meek souls who bear with all manner of offenses and indignities without giving way to anger! Their prayer is acceptable to God, says Holy Scripture (Jdth. 9:16); that is, it will always be heard. "Heaven," says Father Alvarez, "is, in a particular manner, the home and country of those who on earth are despised and trampled under foot." Indeed it is to these, and not to the proud who are honored and esteemed by the world, that the possession of the Kingdom of Heaven is promised. The Royal Psalmist assures us that the meek will not only possess happiness in the life to come, but even in this life: "They shall delight in abundance of peace." (Ps. 36:11).

St. Teresa says that she seemed to experience a more than ordinary love for those who spoke ill of her. In the acts of Canonization we read that by injuries one could obtain her love in an especial degree. To such meekness we can never attain without deep humility, a humble opinion of ourselves, and a desire to be treated with contempt. Pride is angry and vindictive because of the high opinion we have of ourselves and the craving for honors that we think we deserve.

The spirit of God is a spirit of meekness. "My spirit is sweet as honey." (Ecclus. 24:27). St. Francis de Sales, a master and model of holy meekness, says: "Humble meekness is the virtue of virtues, which our Divine Redeemer has most urgently recommended to us; therefore we must practice it everywhere and at all times." Meekness must be exercised especially towards the poor and the sick; towards the poor because, on account of their poverty, they are often harshly treated; towards the sick because they suffer so much and are often left without assistance. Superiors should act with meekness towards their subjects, and when giving an order, they should ask rather than command. St. Vincent de Paul says that superiors have no better means of winning the affection and obedience of their subjects than by meekness.

This was also the opinion of St. Jane Chantal. "I have tried all kinds of treatment," she says; "the mild and patient is the best." "Nothing is so edifying," says St. Francis de Sales, "as amiable meekness." On the lips of this servant of God there hovered a continual smile. His countenance, his conversation, his whole being breathed meekness. St. Vincent de Paul declared that he had never known a meeker man than the Bishop of Geneva. He saw in him a living copy of the goodness and kindness of Jesus Christ. Even when, not to burden his conscience, he had to refuse a request, he couched his refusal in such gentleness and love as to win the cheerful assent of the petitioner; and in spite of a refusal, the latter went away contented. He was meek towards everyone, his superiors, his equals and his inferiors; towards the members of his household and towards strangers. He never complained about his servants; seldom did he reprove them, and then always with gentleness. What a contrast between this saint and those who, according to St. Francis' own words, "seem to be angels abroad and devils at home."

MEEK CORRECTION

If you, Christian reader, are called upon to administer a reproof, do so as St. Francis did, with meekness. To correct emphatically is one thing; to reprove harshly is another. To reprehend in a very positive manner is sometimes necessary, when the fault committed is a serious one or when repeated warnings have been in vain. But we must guard against using an angry tone which betrays an absence of self-control; this often does more harm than good. It is this bitter zeal that St. James deprecates so much. Many imagine that the best and only way to treat subordinates is by harsh deportment, to fill them with reverential awe and dread. But St. James, the Apostle, is of quite a different opinion. He says: "If you have bitter zeal, glory not. This is not wisdom descending from above, but earthly, sensual, devilish. But the wisdom that is from above is . . . peaceable, modest, full of mercy and good fruits." (James 3:14, 15, 17). If you are obliged to speak in a stern manner to impress the culprit with the gravity of his fault, at least conclude your remarks with some kind words to take the sting out of the reproof. Like the good Samaritan, you must heal the wound with oil and wine.

When oil is mixed with other liquids it always comes to the top; so you too, says St. Francis de Sales, in all that you do, let meekness and gentleness predominate. If the person you wish to reprove is very much agitated, it is better to wait until he has grown calm; otherwise you only aggravate him the more. If a house is on fire, it is not the proper thing to throw wood on it.

"You know not of what spirit you are." (Luke 9:55). So spoke the Blessed Redeemer to St. John and his brother St. James when they wished Him to chastise the Samaritans. Ah, what sort of a spirit is that! Our Redeemer wished to say: It is not My spirit; My spirit is meekness and gentleness. "The Son of man came not to destroy souls, but to save" (Luke 9:56), and you wish Me to bring about their destruction.

OUR SAVIOUR'S MEEKNESS

With what meekness and gentleness did not Our Lord speak to the woman taken in sin! "Woman," said He, "hath no man condemned thee? Who said: No man, Lord. And Jesus said: Neither will I condemn thee. Go, and now sin no more." (John 8:10–11). With similar meekness He spoke to and converted the Samaritan woman at Jacob's well. At first He merely asked for a drink of water; and then He said: "O didst thou but know who it is that saith to thee: 'Give me to drink!'" (John 4:10). Finally He revealed to her that He was the promised Messias. What touching tenderness our Saviour displayed towards the treacherous Apostle Judas. He permitted him to eat from the same dish with Himself; He knelt and washed his feet; at the very moment when he was consummating his crime our Saviour warned him with these touching words: "Judas, dost thou betray the Son of man with a kiss?" (Luke 22:48). How did He win back St. Peter after the Apostle had denied Him? He did not reproach him. When passing from the house of the high priest, He turned and looked tenderly upon Peter, and that tender look wrought such a conversion in the heart of the Apostle that during the remainder of his life he wept bitterly over the offense he had given his Divine Master.

Meekness accomplishes far more than anger and bitterness. St. Francis de Sales says there is nothing so bitter as a green walnut; put it in preserve, and it becomes sweet and agreeable. In like manner reproofs, however unpleasant they may be in themselves, become acceptable and productive of good results when administered with meekness and love. By reason of his wonderful meekness, St. Francis de Sales could do whatever he wished; he even succeeded in leading the most obstinate sinners back to God. St. Vincent de Paul was animated with a like spirit and he wished it to be the characteristic of his disciples. "Gentleness, love and humility," he was wont to say, "have a wonderful effect in winning the hearts of men and in causing them to do willingly what is opposed to human nature."

You must endeavor to be mild and amiable to everyone, under all circumstances and at all times. "There are many," says St. Bernard, "who are full of sweetness as long as things go their way; but when they meet with contradiction they break forth in fire and flames, and fume like a veritable Vesuvius. They are like the coals that glow beneath the ashes." He who desires to become a saint must live like a lily among thorns; it is always a lily no matter how much the thorns may prick it. In other words he must always be meek and amiable. The exterior of a soul that loves God will reflect the peace that reigns within alike in prosperity and adversity. If we must answer one who offends us, let us do so with meekness. "A mild answer breaketh wrath," says Holy Scripture. (Prov. 15:1). If we are too excited, it is better to remain silent. In the heat of passion it seems right to say everything that comes to the tongue; but when anger has subsided we find we have committed as many faults as we have spoken words.

MEEKNESS TOWARDS ONESELF

Should we have the misfortune to commit a fault, we must exercise meekness even towards ourselves. To be angry with oneself after committing a fault is not a sign of humility, but of secret pride; it shows that we do not regard ourselves as the weak and wretched creatures that we really are. St. Aloysius said: "The devil likes to fish in troubled waters, where we can distinguish nothing." If a soul is distracted and disturbed it is very hard for it to recognize God and its duties. When, therefore, we have committed a fault, we must turn to the Lord with humility and confidence, beg Him for pardon and say with St. Catherine of Genoa: "Lord, see, here is fruit from my own garden! But pardon me, I beg Thee! I repent from my heart of having offended Thee; I will do so no more; give me the aid of Thy holy grace." "Never," says St. Francis de Sales, "permit anger to enter the soul under any pretext whatever; for once the violent passion has found lodgment in the heart, it is not in our power to banish it."

Seek to control the emotions of anger at once by remaining silent, or by thinking of something else. Do as the Apostles did when they were tossed about by the stormy sea; they had instant recourse to their Divine Master; He alone can still the storms of the human heart. If in consequence of weakness, anger has entered your heart, do all in your power to regain your composure and act humbly and meekly towards him who was the occasion of your angry feelings. St. Francis tells us that it cost him much labor to overcome his two predominant passions, anger and love. To conquer his angry passion he struggled for twelve long years. With regard to love, he changed its object, detaching himself entirely from creatures and giving his whole love to God.

It was a practice with the Saints during prayer and meditation to bring to mind all the annoyance and obstacles they were apt to encounter in the course of the day, and to prepare themselves in advance to endure them with meekness and humility. Thus they were enabled to put into practice the counsel of their gentle Saviour: "Learn of me, because I am meek, and humble of heart: and you shall find rest to your souls." (Matt. 11:29).

Chapter IX

Mortification

"He that hateth his life in this world, keepeth it unto life eternal."—John 12:25

The virtue of mortification is twofold, exterior and interior. Exterior mortification consists in doing and suffering what is opposed to the exterior senses, and in depriving oneself of what is agreeable to them. In as far as it is necessary to avoid sin, every Christian is bound to practice mortification. With regard to those things which we may lawfully enjoy, mortification is not obligatory, but it is very useful and meritorious. For those, however, who are striving after perfection, mortification, even in things that are lawful, is absolutely necessary. As poor children of Adam, we must fight till our dying day; "For the flesh lusteth against the spirit, and the spirit against the flesh, for these are contrary, one to another: so that you do not the things that you would." (Gal. 5:17).

It is proper to animals to gratify their senses; it is characteristic of angels to do the Will of God. From this a learned author concludes that we become angels when we strive to do God's Will, but we become like animals when we seek to gratify our senses. Either the soul must subject the body or the body will make the soul its slave. Accordingly, we must treat our body as a rider treats a wild horse; he draws the reins tight, lest he should be thrown off. A physician at times prescribes medicines that are very distasteful to the patient, and he strictly forbids injurious foods and drinks, though the patient may desire them. He would be a cruel physician indeed who could be dissuaded from administering medicines because his patient objected on account of their being bitter, and who would allow the sick man to eat and drink what he pleased. How much greater is the cruelty of the sensual man who strives to avoid everything that is disagreeable or painful to his body in this life, and thereby puts both body and soul in the greatest danger of suffering incomparably greater pains for all eternity. "This false love," says St. Bernard, "destroys the true love we should have for our body."

Such misplaced sympathy is in reality only cruelty; for while we spare the body we kill the soul. The same Saint, addressing those worldly-minded people who ridicule the servants of God for mortifying themselves, makes use of the following words: "Yes, we are cruel, if you will, towards our bodies when we afflict them with penance; but you are far more cruel towards yourselves when you gratify your sensual cravings, for by so doing you condemn both body and soul to an eternity of frightful torments." Our Lord once said to St. Francis of Assisi: "If you desire Me, take the bitter things of life as sweet and the sweet as bitter." It is useless to assert, as some do, that perfection does not consist in chastising the body, but in mortifying the will. To this Pinamonti replies: "If the vineyard does not bear fruit because it is surrounded by a hedge of thorns, at least the hedge helps to preserve the fruit, for Holy Scripture says: 'Where there is no hedge, the possession shall be spoiled.'" (Ecclus. 36:27).

St. Aloysius Gonzaga had very poor health. Nevertheless, he was so intent on crucifying his body that he sought for nothing but mortification and works of penance. One day someone said to him that sanctity did not consist in these things, but in the renunciation of self-will. He meekly replied in the words of the Gospel:

"These things you ought to have done, and not to leave those undone." (Matt. 23:23). By this he meant to say: Although it is necessary to mortify the will, we must also mortify the body to keep it in check and subject to reason. On this account the Apostle said: "I chastise my body and bring it into subjection." (1 Cor. 9:27). If the body is not mortified, it is very difficult to make it obedient to the law of God.

WE OURSELVES OUR WORST ENEMY

It is certainly true that the world and the devil are great enemies to our salvation; but the greatest enemy of all is our own body because it is always with us. "The enemy that dwells with us in the same house," says St. Bernard, "injures us most." A fort has no more dangerous enemies than those within, for it is harder to protect oneself from these than from the enemy without. While worldly-minded people are intent solely on gratifying their bodies by the pleasures of sense, souls that love God think only of mortifying themselves as much as they can. St. Peter of Alcantara thus addressed his body: "Be assured of the fact that in this life I will give you no rest; afflictions are your lot; when we are in Heaven we shall enjoy a rest without end." In the same spirit St. Mary Magdalen de Pazzi acted, and shortly before her death she could say she did not remember ever having found pleasure in anything except God.

SELF-DENIAL

But, you will say, I have a weak constitution and poor health, and my confessor forbids me to practice works of penance. Very well, obey him; but at least bear patiently with the discomforts and fatigue resulting from your bodily condition; try not to complain of the inclemency of the weather and the excessive heat and cold. If you are unable to practice works of penance, at least abstain occasionally from some lawful pleasure. When St. Francis Borgia was out hunting, at the moment the falcon would seize its prey he used to cast down his eyes, to deprive himself of the pleasure such a sight would afford him. If you deny your body lawful pleasures, it is not apt to seek unlawful ones; but if you indulge in all the lawful enjoyments you will soon cross the line into forbidden territory. A great servant of God, Vincent Carafa, S.J., says that the Lord has given us the joys and pleasures of this world not only that we may enjoy them, but also that we might have an opportunity of making a sacrifice, by depriving ourselves of them for love of Him. Poisons properly compounded, and taken in very small quantity, are sometimes beneficial to the health of the body, but they are and always will be poisons. And so it is with pleasures; they must be indulged in with great precaution and moderation and solely with the view of serving God more faithfully.

Moreover, we must be on our guard lest anxiety and solicitude for our bodily welfare endanger the health of the soul. "The sickness of the body," says St. Bernard, "excites my compassion, but the sickness of the soul causes me greater affliction because it is much more dangerous." We are very apt to make our bodily ailments a pretext for exemption from our spiritual duties. "We omit prayer today," says St. Teresa, "because we have a headache; tomorrow because we had a headache, and the next day because we fear we might get one."

ADVANTAGES OF MORTIFICATION

It may be profitable to dwell for a moment on the advantages of mortification, for such a consideration is calculated to inspire us with more courage and generosity. By mortification we may expiate the temporal punishment due to our sins. We are aware of the fact that though the guilt of sin is remitted by a contrite Confession, there still remains a temporal punishment to be endured. If in the present life we neglect to make atonement, we shall have to suffer in the fire of Purgatory. "Except they do penance for their deeds," says Holy Scripture, "they shall be in very great tribulation." (Apoc. 2:22). St. Antonine relates that the choice was offered to a sick man (by his guardian angel) either to suffer three days in Purgatory or to remain two years longer on his sickbed. The patient chose the three days in Purgatory. He had hardly been there an hour when he complained to the angel that instead of a few days he had already spent several years in terrible torments. "What is it you say," replied the angel; "your body is still warm on the deathbed, and you speak of years?" If therefore, Christian soul, you have anything to suffer, say to yourself: This must be my Purgatory; I shall bear this suffering patiently to atone for my sins, and to gain merit for eternal life.

IT ELEVATES THE SOUL

Mortification raises the soul to God. St. Francis de Sales says: "The soul can never ascend to God unless the body is brought into subjection by penance." "Souls that truly love God," says St. Teresa, "have no desire for bodily rest and indulgence." But by mortification we may attain great glory in Heaven. "If contestants," says St. Paul, "abstain from everything that might weaken the body and prevent them from winning a perishable crown, with what greater zeal ought not we to mortify ourselves in order to obtain a priceless and eternal crown!" St. John saw the blessed in Heaven with palm branches in their hands. From this it is evident that to be numbered among the elect we must all be martyrs, either by the sword of the tyrant or by mortification. But "The sufferings of this time are not worthy to be compared with the glory to come, that shall be revealed in us" (Rom. 8:18), and our present tribulations are momentary and light, but they "work for us above measure exceedingly an eternal weight of glory." (2 Cor. 4:17). Let us therefore reanimate our faith. We have but a short time to live on this earth; our true home and eternal rest is beyond the grave. St. Peter says that the blessed are the living stones with which the heavenly Jerusalem is built. But as Holy Church sings in the Divine Office, these stones must be cut and shaped by the chisel of mortification.

INTERIOR MORTIFICATION

Interior mortification consists in restraining our inordinate self-love and self-will. There is a twofold love of self, the one good and the other bad. The former spurs us on to strive for eternal life, for which God has created us; the latter prompts us to seek for the good things of this earth, to the great detriment of our immortal soul. Christ Our Lord has said: "If any man will come after me, let him deny himself." (Matt. 16:24). Now, all the perfection of a soul consists in this very self-denial, for St. Augustine says, "The less one seeks to gratify the passions, the more one truly loves God, and when one desires nothing but God, one's love of God is perfect." In the present condition of our sinful nature, it is impossible to be entirely free from the promptings of self-love. Jesus Christ alone among men and the Blessed Virgin Mary among women were entirely exempt. As for all the other Saints, they have had to battle with their inordinate inclinations. Interior mortification, therefore, consists principally in restraining and keeping in check these inordinate inclinations of self-love. The soul has other enemies, it is true, but the worst enemy of all is self-love.

According to St. Mary Magdalen de Pazzi, "Self-love is like the worm that gnaws at the root and destroys not only the fruit, but even the very life of the plant." The same Saint adds: "The traitor that we have to fear most is self-love, for self-love betrays us as Judas betrayed Our Lord with a kiss. He who conquers self-love has conquered all." Pray, therefore, without ceasing, to the Lord: O God, do not let me fall a prey to my passions, which rob me of Thy holy fear and of reason itself. "Man's life on earth is a warfare." (Job 7:1). He who encounters an enemy in battle must have his weapons in hand to defend himself; if he neglects to fight, he is lost. No matter how many victories we may have won, we cannot afford to lay down our arms; for our passions, in spite of repeated defeats, are never entirely destroyed.

They are like weeds, says St. Bernard, that crop out again as often as they are cut off; even when you think you have rooted them out entirely, they soon appear again. In the struggle with our passions, the most we can hope to attain is that their attacks become less frequent and less violent, and we ourselves better able to overcome them. One day a monk complained to the Abbot Theodore that he had fought for eight long years against his passions and had not as yet succeeded in subduing them. The Abbot replied: "My brother, you complain of a war of eight years; I have spent sixty years in solitude and there was not a single day of that time but I was disquieted by some passion or other." The passions, therefore, will always molest us; but, as St. Gregory says, "It is a different thing to see these wild beasts prowling around us and to hear their ferocious howl than to have them in our very heart and to suffer them to strangle us."

SELF-CONQUEST

Our heart is a garden in which wild and noxious weeds continue to grow. We must therefore have the hoe of mortification always in hand to remove this noxious growth, otherwise the garden will soon be choked with thorns and thistles. "Overcome yourself," was a favorite saying with St. Ignatius of Loyola. It was always on his lips; again and again he returned to it when addressing his religious brethren. "Overcome your self-love; break your self-will," he would say. The reason why so few of those who practice mental prayer become saints is because so few are intent upon over-coming themselves. Of a hundred persons who practice mental prayer, more than ninety follow their own head.

Therefore, the Saint placed greater value on a single act of self-denial than on a whole hour's prayer filled with spiritual consolation. "Of what benefit is it to a fortress," says the Abbot Gilbert, "that the gates are closed if hunger, the enemy within, lays low the occupants?" He wished to say: Of what use is it to mortify the exterior senses and perform many exercises of piety if we harbor some passion in our heart and refuse to give up our own will?

St. Francis Borgia said that prayer introduces the love of God into the heart, but mortification prepares the way by removing everything that might prove an obstacle or hindrance to it. If you wish to fill a vase with water you must first empty out the earth that is in it, otherwise there will be a disagreeable mixture. Regarding the relation of interior mortification to prayer, Father Balthasar Alvarez says: "Prayer without mortification is either a delusion, or will soon come to an end." St. Ignatius tells us that a mortified soul is more intimately united to God in one quarter of an hour than an unmortified person in many hours of prayer. And if the Saint heard it said of anyone that he prayed much, he would add: "That is a sign that he is very mortified."

Many Christians perform acts of devotion, go frequently to Holy Communion, fast and spend much time at prayer, but they neglect to mortify their passions, and harbor feelings of revenge and aversion, and entertain dangerous attachments. They make no effort to bear with contradictions, to give up certain associations and to be subject to obedience and the Will of God. What progress can such hope to make on the way to perfection? They always have the same faults, and according to St. Augustine they are outside the right way. "They run well," says the Saint, "but outside the path." "Watch over thyself," says Thomas à Kempis, "stir up thyself, admonish thyself; and whatsoever becometh of others, neglect not thyself. The greater violence thou offerest to thyself the greater progress thou wilt make." (Im. Bk. 1, 24).

I have not the slightest intention to underestimate the value of vocal prayer, works of penance and other spiritual exercises; but they must be performed with this end in view, to obtain the victory over your passions. All exercises of piety are nothing else but means to arrive at virtue. Consequently at Holy Communion, during meditation, while visiting the Blessed Sacrament and performing other acts of devotion we must always ask God for the grace to be humble, mortified, obedient and conformed to His holy will. To act only from self-love is a fault in every Christian; but it is a greater fault in him who has received a greater measure of grace and is on that account bound to strive more earnestly after perfection. "By means of self-denial," says Lactantius, "God calls men to eternal life; by the gratification of self-love Satan calls them to eternal death."

St. Joseph Calasanctius used to say: "The day spent without mortification is a day lost." In order to teach us the value and necessity of mortification, our Blessed Lord chose to live a mortified life, a life without sensible consolation, a life of sorrow and shame. "Having joy set before him," says the Apostle, "he endured the cross, despising the shame." (Heb. 12:2). "Go through the whole life of Jesus Christ" says St. Bernard, "you will always find Him suffering on the cross." St. Catherine of Siena remarks: "As a mother takes bitter medicine to cure her sick child, so during His life on earth Our Lord drank the chalice of sufferings to cure our poor sick souls."

SELF-WILL

There is no obstacle more harmful in striving after perfection than the gratification of self-will. "If," says St. Bernard, "you can induce men to give up their self-will, there is no Hell for them to fear." According to St. Peter Damian, self-will destroys all the virtues. "As the will of God is the source of all good," says St. Anselm, "the will of man is the origin of all evil." "He," says St. Bernard, "who constitutes himself a master and follows the suggestions of self-will subjects himself to a veritable fool."

The devil, as St. Augustine remarks, became what he is by self-will. Therefore, in his war against pious souls, his most effective and deadly weapon is their self-will. Cassian relates that the Abbot Achilles, when asked by a disciple what weapons the devil employed in attacking the souls that are consecrated to God, replied: Against the great ones of this world, he uses pride; against men of business, avarice; against the young, incontinence; but against those who are given to piety, his principal weapon is self-will. The Abbot Pastor expresses the same idea in different words: "When we follow our own will, the devil has no need of assailing us, for our self-will then takes the place of the devil, and indeed of the worst that there is." The Holy Ghost admonishes us: "Turn away from thy own will. If thou give to thy soul her desires, she will make thee a joy to thy enemies." (Ecclus. 18:30–31). An action has its greatest value from the obedience through which it is performed. The worst feature of any action is when it is prompted by self-will.

Consequently, says Trithemius, the devil hates nothing more than obedience, for, in the words of St. Teresa, "The devil well knows that on obedience the salvation of our souls depends. This is why he tries so hard to prevent it." It was the custom of St. Philip Neri to exhort all his penitents to practice renunciation of their own will, for in this, he used to say, true sanctity consists. "The more you take away from your self-will, the more you add to virtue," says St. Jerome. "In the sight of God," says St. Coletta, "the renunciation of self-will is more meritorious than the sacrifice of all the riches of the world."

"I wish for very little," says St. Francis de Sales, "and for this little I have but feeble desire." He meant to say that in his desires his own will was never considered, but simply the Will of God; so that he was prepared to give up everything as soon as he saw that it was not in conformity with the divine Will. "O what sweetness," says St. Mary Magdalen de Pazzi, "there is in the words 'The Will of God.'"

If you, Christian soul, desire to become holy and enjoy uninterrupted peace, strive as often as you can to mortify your will. Do nothing for your own satisfaction, but everything to please God. To this end renounce all vain desires and inordinate inclinations. Worldly-minded people are intent upon following their own will as much as they possibly can; it is the constant aim of the Saints to mortify their will, and they seek opportunities for doing so. St. Andrew Avellino made a vow always to oppose his own will. Make it a practice at least every day to perform a few acts of self-denial.

Let us conclude with the words which Father Torres wrote to a devout person to encourage her in the practice of self-denial: "As God has given you an opportunity to suffer and endure abandonment, endeavor to increase His love in your heart, a love that is as strong as death. May this love detach you from all creatures and from your very self in order that nothing may hinder you in clinging to your Lord with all your thoughts, desires and inclinations. Do all for Him and in union with Him. Before your crucified Saviour make a daily renunciation of all the inclinations and attachments you find within your soul. Protest that you desire no other honor but the shame of Jesus Christ; no other treasure but His love; no other comforts but His Cross; no other object but Himself, your Lord and God."

Chapter X

Recollection

"Having dismissed the multitude, he went into a mountain alone to pray."—Matt. 14:23

To preserve recollection of spirit or the constant union of the soul with God, three things are necessary: solitude, silence, and the recollection of the presence of God. It was these three things which the angel of God referred to when, addressing St. Arsenius, he said: "Flee, be silent and rest." In other words: seek solitude, practice silence, and rest in God by keeping the thought of His presence ever before you.

Souls that love God feel a strong attraction for solitude, for they know that God converses familiarly with those who shun the noise and distractions of the world. "O blessed solitude," exclaims St. Jerome, "in which God with loving condescension deals familiarly with chosen souls!" God does not speak in those places where time is squandered in loud laughter and idle talk. "The Lord is not in the earthquake" (3 Kgs. 19:11), but He says, on the contrary, in the words of the prophet Osee: "I will lead her into the wilderness and I will speak to her heart." (Osee 2:14). God speaks to the soul in solitude, and by His words the heart is inflamed with divine love. "My soul melted when my beloved spoke," said the spouse in the Canticle (5:6).

St. Eucherius relates that a person who desired to be perfect once asked a spiritual director what he had to do, and this was the answer he received: "Solitude is the place where man finds God. In solitude, virtue is easily preserved; in intercourse with the world it is easily lost." St. Bernard tells us that he learned more about God and divine things in solitude under the oaks and beeches than from the books and schools of the learned. For this reason the Saints felt an irresistible yearning to leave the noise and bustle of the world and retire into solitude; for this reason the mountains and forests and caves were inexpressibly dear to them. In the prophecy of Isaias we read: "The land that was desolate and impassable shall be glad, and the wilderness shall rejoice, and shall flourish like the lily. It shall bud forth and blossom, and shall rejoice with joy and praise: the glory of Libanus is given to it; the beauty of Carmel, and Saron, they shall see the glory of the Lord, and the beauty of our God." (Is. 35:1). In other words, for interior souls, solitude is the source of abundant delights, for it is there they look upon and contemplate the majesty and beauty of God.

THE THOUGHT OF GOD

In order to remain united to God, we must endeavor to keep alive within us a vivid recollection of Him and of the immeasurable goods He bestows on them that love Him. By constant intercourse with the world, these spiritual truths are apt to become obscured in the maze of earthly thoughts and considerations, and piety vanishes from the heart. Worldly-minded people shun solitude, and it is quite natural for them to do so; for it is in retirement that they are troubled with qualms of conscience. They seek the society and excitement of the world so that the voice of conscience may be drowned in the noise that reigns there. Those, on the contrary, whose conscience is at rest, love solitude and retirement; and when at times they are obliged by circumstances to appear in the noisy world, they are ill at ease and feel altogether out of their element.

It is true, man naturally loves the society of his fellow man; but what can be found more beautiful than the society of God? "His conversation hath no bitterness," says Holy Scripture, "and his company no tediousness, but joy and gladness." (Wis. 8:16). A life of solitude is not a life of sadness; it is rather a foretaste of Heaven; it is the beginning of the life of the blessed whose sole happiness is found in the love and praise of God. This is what St. Jerome said when he fled from the society of Rome and hid himself in the grotto of Bethlehem: "Solitude is my Heaven," he wrote. In solitude the Saints seem to be entirely alone, but this is not so. St. Bernard said: "Never am I less alone than when alone"; for when I am alone I am with God, who gives me greater joy than the society of all creatures could afford. If the Saints seem to be sad, in reality they are not so. Because the world sees them deprived of all earthly joys and pleasures, it regards them as most unhappy; and yet the very opposite is the case.

According to the words of the Apostle, they enjoy a constant and immeasurable peace. (2 Thess. 3:16). Now, in order to find this delightful solitude it is not necessary to withdraw into a desert and live in a cave; you can find it in your home and in the midst of your family. Busy yourself with the outside world only in as far as the duties of your state, obedience, or charity require, and you will be living in that solitude that best accords with your circumstances and that God requires of you. In the midst of the weightiest affairs of state, King David knew how to find a solitude: "Behold I fled away and dwelt in solitude." (Ps. 54:8). St. Philip Neri for some time entertained the desire to retire into a desert, but the Lord commanded him not to leave the city of Rome, and to live there as if he were in a hermitage.

SOLITUDE OF THE SPIRIT

Hitherto we have spoken of the solitude and retirement of the body; there is also a solitude of the soul, and the latter is more necessary than the former, for St. Gregory says: "Of what use is the solitude of the body without the solitude of the spirit?" Of what benefit is it, the Saint wishes to say, to live in a desert if the soul clings to the things of this earth? "A soul that is free from earthly attachments," says St. Peter Chrysologus, "finds solitude even on the streets and in public places." Of what advantage is it to remain quiet at home or in church if our heart is centered on the things of earth, and the noise of these earthly things prevents us from hearing the voice of God? One day the Lord said to St.

Teresa: "Oh, how gladly would I speak to many souls! But the world makes so much noise in their hearts that they cannot hear My voice. Would that they might retire a little from the world!" In what does solitude of the heart consist? It consists in banishing from the heart all desires and inclinations that are not for God, and in performing our actions simply with God's good pleasure in view. The Psalmist expresses this truth in the following words: "What have I in heaven, and besides thee what do I desire upon earth? Thou art the God of my heart and the God that is my portion forever." (Ps. 72:25–26). In one word, the solitude of the heart consists in being able to say: "My God, Thee alone do I desire and nothing else."

HOW TO FIND GOD

Many complain that they are unable to find God, but to such St. Teresa replies: "Tear your heart away from everything else; then seek God and you will surely find Him." If a crystal vase is filled with earth, the rays of the sun cannot penetrate it. The light of God cannot illumine a heart that is full of attachments for the joys, the pleasures and the honors of this world. "When thou shalt pray," says Our Lord, "enter into thy chamber, and having shut the door, pray to thy Father in secret." (Matt. 6:6). In other words, to be united to God in prayer, man must enter into his own heart—which St. Augustine says is the chamber mentioned by Our Lord—and shut out all earthly attachments and inclinations. It is not to be supposed that solitude and retirement are synonymous with idleness. Many live in retirement, but it is an inactive and useless retirement of which they shall have to render an account. Devout souls, on the contrary, are like bees that are never tired preparing honey for their cells. No time must be lost, but every moment employed in praying, in reading or in performing the duties of your state of life.

"Idleness is the mother of vice," says the proverb, and the foundation of this proverb is the words of Holy Scripture: "Idleness hath taught much evil." (Ecclus. 33:29). According to St. Bonaventure, the idle man is tortured by a thousand temptations, while the man that is busily occupied has comparatively few. We cannot pray all the time; therefore, we must devote ourselves to work. In the life of St. Mary Magdalen de Pazzi it is said that she did more work than four lay sisters together.

It would be an error to suppose that work is injurious to health; on the contrary, it is very conducive to our bodily welfare. Work is moreover an effective remedy against temptations. One day St. Anthony the hermit was assailed by numerous temptations and with a sudden aversion for his solitude; he scarcely knew which way to turn. An angel appeared and led him into the garden; thereupon he picked up a hoe and began to cultivate the ground. Afterwards he prayed for a while, and then returned to work. From this the Saint learned how he was to act, and the subsequent interchange of prayer and labor made his solitude very agreeable, while at the same time it protected him from many temptations.

But even labor need not prevent us from prayer. One day St. Bernard saw a monk praying while doing his work. "Continue in this way, my brother," said he, "and after death you will have no Purgatory." While our hands are occupied with external occupations, our heart can be fixed on God. The good intention we make in performing our labors sanctifies them in the sight of God and even makes of labor a prayer, for prayer has been called "the raising of the mind and heart to God."

SILENCE

Silence is one of the principal means to attain the spirit of prayer and to fit oneself for uninterrupted intercourse with God. It is hard to find a truly pious person who talks much. But they who have the spirit of prayer love silence, which has deservedly been called a protectress of innocence, a shield against temptations and a fruitful source of prayer. Silence promotes recollection and awakens good thoughts in the heart. According to St. Bernard, it forces the soul, as it were, to think of God and heavenly things. For this reason the Saints of God were great lovers of silence.

In the prophecy of Isaias we read: "The work of justice shall be peace, and the service of justice quietness, and security forever." (Is. 32:17). On the one hand, silence preserves us from many sins by removing the occasion of uncharitable talk, rancor and curiosity; on the other it aids us in the attainment of many virtues. For example: What an excellent opportunity we have for the practice of humility by modestly keeping silence while others speak! How well we may practice mortification by refraining from relating something we very much desire to tell! What a splendid chance to exercise meekness by not replying to unjust accusations and insults!

Unrestrained and immoderate talking, on the other hand, has many disastrous consequences. If devotion is preserved by silence, it is certainly lost by much talking. A person may be ever so recollected at meditation; if afterwards he does not restrain his tongue, he will be as distracted as if he had made no meditation at all.

If you open the doors of a furnace, the heat will escape. "Guard against much talking," says St. Dorotheus, "for it puts to flight devout thoughts and recollection in God." It is certain that a person who talks much with creatures, will converse little with God, and on His part God will speak little to such a one, for He says: "I will lead her into the wilderness and will speak to her heart." (Osee 2:14). "In the multitude of words," says the Holy Ghost, "there shall not want sin, but he that refraineth his lips is most wise." (Prov. 10:19). St. James says that "the tongue is a world of iniquity" (James 3:6), for as a learned author remarks, very many sins are occasioned by talking or listening to the talk of others.

Ah, how many souls will be lost on judgment day because they have not watched over their tongue! "The man full of tongue," says the Psalmist, "shall wander about without a guide" (Ps. 139), and go into a thousand and one byways with no hope of returning. "He that keepeth his mouth, keepeth his soul," says the Wise Man, "but he that hath no guard on his speech shall meet with evils." (Prov. 13:3). And St. James writes: "If any man offend not in word, the same is a perfect man." (James 3:2). For he who for the love of God keeps silence will likewise be given to meditation, spiritual reading and prayer before the Blessed Sacrament. It is impossible, says St. Mary Magdalen de Pazzi, for one who does not love silence to take pleasure in divine things; before long he will throw himself into the very midst of the pleasures of the world.

THE VALUE OF SILENCE

The virtue of silence does not consist in never speaking, but in keeping silent when there is no good reason to speak. Solomon says: "There is a time to keep silence and a time to speak." (Eccles. 3:7). In reference to these words, St. Gregory of Nyssa remarks: "The time to keep silence is mentioned first, because by silence we learn the art of speaking well." When therefore should a Christian, who desires to become holy, be silent, and when should he speak? He should be silent when it is not necessary to speak and he should speak when necessity or charity requires it. St. Chrysostom gives the following rule: "Speak only when it is more useful to speak than to be silent."

St. Arsenius acknowledges that he often regretted having spoken, but never, having kept silence. St. Ephrem says: "Speak much with God but little with men." If in your presence unbecoming and sinful language is used, leave the company if it is possible to do so. At least cast down your eyes and remain silent, or lead the conversation to some other topic, thus making a silent protest against such unsavory talk. Be not over eager to hear the news; curiosity leads to many faults. The Abbot John used to say: "He who would hold his tongue in check, must close his ears by suppressing the desire to hear the news." And when you do speak, weigh well what you intend to say. "Put your words in the balance," says the Holy Ghost. (Ecclus. 28:29). St. Francis de Sales quaintly remarked: "To avoid faults in speech we must have the lips buttoned together, so that while unbuttoning them we may think of what we are going to say."

THE PRESENCE OF GOD

A powerful aid in preserving recollection is the remembrance of the presence of God. Not only does it conduce to recollection of spirit, but it is also one of the most effective means of advancing in the spiritual life; it helps us to avoid sin; it spurs us on in the practice of virtue, and it brings about an intimate union of the soul with God.

There is no more excellent means of quieting the passions and of resisting the temptation to sin than the thought of the presence of God. St. Thomas says: "If we thought of the presence of God at all times we would never, or very seldom, do anything to displease Him." According to St. Jerome, the recollection of God's presence closes the door on all sins. For, if in the presence of our rulers, our parents or superiors, we do not care to transgress their commands, how could we violate the commandments of God if we remembered that His eyes were upon us?

St. Ambrose tells us that during a sacrifice which Alexander the Great was offering in the temple, a certain page who held a lighted torch allowed it to burn his hand rather than be guilty of irreverence by letting it fall. And the holy Doctor adds: If respect for the presence of the king could overcome the impulse of nature itself in this boy, how much more ought not the thought of the presence of God to prevail with a faithful soul in overcoming temptations and in suffering every imaginable torture rather than offend God before His very eyes.

Men fall into sin because they lose sight of the presence of God. "The cause of all evil," says St. Teresa, "lies in the fact that we do not think of the presence of God, but imagine Him far away from us." A man who loses sight of the presence of God will easily become a prey to sinful and sensual desires and have no strength to resist them.

On the other hand, by the thought of God's ever vigilant eye upon them, the Saints have had strength to resist and overcome all the attacks of the evil one. It was this thought that gave the chaste Susanna courage to spurn the wicked advances of the men who tried to seduce her and even threatened her with death. "It is better for me," she said, "to fall into your hands without doing evil, than to sin in the sight of the Lord." (Dan.13:23). The same thought converted a wicked woman who dared to tempt St. Ephrem to sin. The Saint replied that if she wished to sin, she would have to go with him into the public square. "But," she inquired, "how is it possible to commit sin in the presence of so many people?" "And how is it possible," rejoined the Saint, "to commit sin in the presence of God, who sees us everywhere?" At these words the poor sinner broke out into tears, threw herself at his feet and begged the Saint's pardon, beseeching him to lead her into the way of salvation. The Saint secured her admission into a convent, where she led an edifying life and bewailed her sins to her dying day.

Something similar is narrated in the life of the Abbot Paphnutius. A certain sinful woman named Thais thought she might induce him to do wrong by saying that no one but God would be a witness to the deed. The Saint replied in a very earnest tone: "You believe, then, that God really sees you, and nevertheless you wish to sin?" These words made such an impression on her that she began to conceive a horror of her wicked life. She brought all the jewels and clothing she had secured by a life of sin, heaped them together in the public marketplace, and set them on fire. Then she entered a convent and fasted for three years on bread and water, constantly repeating the following words: "Thou who hast created me, have mercy on me." At the end of three years she died a holy death. It was shortly after revealed to a disciple of the Abbot Anthony that the happy penitent had merited a crown of glory among the Saints. Therefore St. Chrysostom says: "If we keep ourselves in the presence of God we shall neither think nor say nor do what is wrong, convinced as we are that God is the witness of all our thoughts and words and actions."

A GREAT INCENTIVE

As far as the practice of the Christian virtues is concerned, the recollection of God's presence affords us a powerful stimulus. How bravely will not soldiers fight in the presence of their general! The thought that his eyes are upon them, and that he will either reward or punish them, animates their courage and strength in a high degree. If we, too, would bear in mind that in all we do God's eyes are upon us, would we not try to do everything well and from the purest of intentions? St. Basil once said: "If you happened to be in the presence of a prince and a peasant, would you not naturally try to make your conduct agreeable to the prince, regardless of what the peasant might like you to do; in a similar manner, he who walks in the presence of God is little concerned about what creatures may think or say;

his whole concern is to please God, who sees his every action."

Union of the soul with God is the third happy result of walking constantly in His presence. Love is always strengthened by the presence of the object loved. If this is the case with human beings, in spite of the many defects their presence must needs reveal, how much more so will it be between the soul and God. The more we walk in the presence of God, the better we recognize those beautiful qualities that are calculated to increase and strengthen His love in our hearts.

But in order to remain intimately united to God it is not sufficient to make a morning and evening meditation. St. Chrysostom says: If you remove boiling water from the stove, it will soon cool off. So it is with the human soul; to keep the fire of God's love aglow, the thought of His presence must be constantly before us. Blessed Henry Suso devoted himself to this holy exercise with the greatest zeal and eventually reached a most intimate union with God. Of St. Gertrude, Our Lord once said to St. Mechtildis: "This holy soul that I love so much, walks continually in My presence and is solely intent upon doing My will and performing her actions for My greater glory." David was filled with joy and consolation whenever he thought of God: "I remembered God and was delighted." (Ps. 76:4).

HOW TO WALK IN GOD'S PRESENCE

Now a good means of walking in God's presence is to picture Our Lord as present with us wherever we may happen to be. We may think of Him at times as a little babe in the crib of Bethlehem; as a poor exile on His way to Egypt; as an apprentice in the workshop of Nazareth; a man of sorrows who was condemned a criminal to suffer and die; as scourged and crowned and crucified. St. Teresa praised this practice very much. It is necessary to observe, however, that in this pious exercise we must avoid all straining of the imagination, which is apt to be very fatiguing and might possibly be injurious.

Another and better means of walking in the presence of God is based on the truths of holy faith. It consists in seeing God with the eyes of faith and being thoroughly persuaded that He is present and a witness of our actions. It matters not that we are unable to see Him with our bodily eyes; we cannot see the air around us, and we never doubt for a moment that it exists and that without it we could not possibly live. We do not see God, but faith tells us He is everywhere present. The Apostle St. Paul says: "In him we live and move and are." (Acts 17:28). This is an easy practice and is not tiring to the mind. It is sufficient to make little acts of faith such as the following: My God, I firmly believe that Thou art here present. With this may be joined acts of love, of conformity and of good intention.

Still another beautiful practice is that of seeing God in His creatures. The beauties of nature such as the rising and setting of the sun, a magnificent landscape, a majestic river, a garden of beautiful flowers are so many reflexes of the beauty of the Creator. The thought of a learned or handsome or holy man can lead us to admire the wisdom and beauty and sanctity of God and return Him thanks for permitting His creatures to share in His holy attributes.

The most perfect method, however, of keeping alive the thought of God's presence consists in beholding God within our very selves. It is not necessary to ascend to Heaven to find the Lord God; we need only to recollect ourselves, and we shall find Him within us. He who, at prayer, pictures the Lord at a great distance from him is preparing for himself a source of abundant distractions. St. Teresa says: "I never really knew what it meant to pray well until the Lord Himself taught me the proper way to converse with Him. I entered within my very self and found this practice exceedingly profitable for my soul."

God is within us in a different manner from what He is in other creatures; in us He dwells as the Lord in His temple and in His house. "Know you not," says St. Paul, "that you are the temple of God, and that the Spirit of God dwelleth in you?" (1 Cor. 3:16). And our Divine Saviour Himself has said: "If anyone love me, he will keep my word, and my Father will love him, and we will come to him and make our abode with him." (John 14:23). Endeavor, therefore, to reanimate your faith in this consoling truth. Humble yourself profoundly before so exalted a Majesty who deigns to dwell within you. Excite yourself to frequent acts of confidence, of oblation and of love towards the boundless goodness of God. St. Catherine of Siena tells us that she built a little cell in the innermost part of her soul; there she entertained herself in loving converse with her God. Once, when speaking of this presence of God in our heart, St. Teresa said: "Those who withdraw into the little heaven of their soul, where He who created them is enthroned, can be certain that in a brief space of time they will have advanced far on the road to perfection."

The happiness of the elect in Heaven consists in seeing and loving God. Our happiness here on earth must likewise consist in loving and seeing Our Lord, not indeed face to face as the Saints and angels do, but by means of the light of faith. Thus we begin in this valley of tears, this earthly exile, the life of the blessed in Heaven, a life of endless joy in the fruition of the vision of God.

Chapter XI

Prayer

"We ought always to pray and not to faint."—Luke 18:1

According to the teaching of the angelic St. Thomas, the worship of God takes the first place in the order of moral virtues; it is occupied more with God and leads us nearer to Him than the others. For every Christian, therefore, who is striving after perfection it must be a matter of no little concern to make this virtue his own in the highest degree. Now the easiest means of doing so, a means that we can employ at all times and in all places, is found in prayer. Whether it be the prayer of praise or thanksgiving or impenetration or propitiation, we are worshipping God, for every prayer is a humble acknowledgment of the greatness or goodness or fidelity or mercy of God.

Vocal prayer, or prayer pronounced by the lips, is very pleasing to God because by it the endless Majesty of God is acknowledged and glorified. "The sacrifice of praise shall glorify me," says the Lord by the mouth of the prophet David, "and there is the way by which I will show him the salvation of God." (Ps. 49:23). St. Mary Magdalen de Pazzi was almost beside herself with joy when she heard the sound of the bell that called the community to prayer. She left everything at once to devote herself to this holy exercise, for she felt that she was performing the function of an angel in proclaiming the praises of God.

QUALITIES OF VOCAL PRAYER

In order, however, that vocal prayer may tend to God's glory and our own salvation, it must be accompanied by attention and devotion. Not only the pronouncing of the words, says St. Gregory, but also the devotion of the heart is required for true prayer; for in the eyes of God, our sentiments are of greater worth than the sound of our voice. If we wish, therefore, to please God we must pray not only with the lips, but also with the heart. How could the Lord, continues the same Saint, hear the prayers of him who knows not what he wants, and does not even wish to be heard? How can you expect the Lord to hear you when you cannot hear yourself? says St. Cyprian. Prayer made with attention and devotion is like sweet-smelling incense that is agreeable to God and wins for us treasures of graces. On the other hand, prayer without recollection is insulting and offensive to God and calls down His wrath on the offender.

If a subject came into the presence of his sovereign, and while petitioning some favor, gazed about and occupied himself with irrelevant matters in such wise that he scarcely knew what he was saying, would not that sovereign be justly offended? For this reason St. Thomas teaches that he who permits his mind to wander about during prayer cannot be excused from sin, because by such conduct he seems to be guilty of contempt of God. The Lord might well say of many Christians what He once said of the Jews: "They honor me with their lips but their heart is far from me." (Matt. 15:8).

It is easy to understand why the devil is so intent upon turning our thoughts towards worldly affairs during prayer. On the one hand, he desires to rob us of the benefit we derive from fervent prayer; and on the other he wishes to make us guilty of disrespect towards

God, and therefore, deserving of punishment. But just on this account we ought to strive most earnestly to pray with the greatest attention and devotion. Before entering the church, let us follow the advice of St. John Chrysostom and dismiss all worldly thoughts. The Holy Ghost exhorts us in the following words: "Before prayer prepare thy soul; and be not as a man that tempteth God." (Ecclus. 18:23). Try to bring yourself to realize that you are going to praise God and to beg for His mercy, both for yourself and for others. Remember that the angels are looking upon you and are standing, as Blessed Herman saw them one day, with golden censers, prepared to offer your prayers and holy affections to God as sweet-smelling incense. The angels that St. John the Evangelist saw held golden vials of incense and odors which were the prayers of the Saints. (Apoc. 5:8). In a word, think before prayer that you are going to converse with God and to treat with Him about some very important affairs. Then the Lord will look upon you with a gracious eye and turn an attentive ear to your petitions.

Offer Him beforehand the prayers you intend to say, and beg Him to preserve you from distractions. During prayer, avoid haste. Many people, when praying, seem to be intent only on reaching the end of their prayers, as if it were a torture that must be endured, but during the shortest possible time. Such irreverent haste can hardly be pleasing to God or profitable to ourselves. "Zeal and fervor," says St. Augustine, "gradually cool off and, like a fire, become extinct unless they are kept alive." Endeavor from time to time to renew your attention while at your prayers and devotions.

Attention during prayer must be both interior and exterior. Exterior attention requires that you abstain from everything that is incompatible with interior recollection. For example, it would hardly be proper during prayer to speak with others or to listen to a conversation that is going on, or to gaze about at every distracting object. Interior attention is threefold: it may be directed to the words you utter, or to their sense, or, finally, to God. Attention is directed to the words when you are careful to pronounce them well; it is directed to the sense of the words when you try to understand their meaning in order to unite suitable affections of the heart with the verbal utterance. You direct your attention to God, and this is the best kind of attention, when during prayer your mind is fixed on God with a view to adore Him, to thank Him, to love Him or to ask Him for His graces.

DISTRACTIONS

As long as you strive to preserve the proper attention at prayer, you need not be disturbed by involuntary distractions; provided you do not consent to them, they can do you no harm. The Lord has compassion on our weakness. Distracting thoughts often enter the mind when we have given no occasion for them whatever. Such thoughts cannot spoil the effects of our prayer. According to the illustrious St. Thomas, even favored souls cannot always remain in the heights of contemplation. The weight of human infirmities bows them down and occasions some involuntary distractions. On the other hand, says the same holy Doctor, he cannot be excused from sin nor expect a reward for his prayer who entertains distractions that are voluntary.

As a good will makes our thoughts worthy of spiritual fruit, says St. Bernard, an indolent will makes them unworthy of the Lord; and therefore, instead of a reward, they receive only punishment. The annals of Citeaux contain the following vision which St. Bernard had one day when at prayer with his religious brethren. At the side of each of the brethren, he saw an angel who stood and wrote. Some of the angels wrote with gold, others with silver, still others with ink, and some with water—while a number held the pen in their hand without writing at all. At the same time God enlightened the Saint to know what this meant: the gold denoted that the prayers of these particular brethren were said with the greatest fervor; the silver indicated that the devotion of others left something to be desired; the writing in ink meant that the words were carefully spoken, but that no devotion accompanied them; the water was intended to show that the words were carelessly pronounced, and little or no attention paid to what was said; finally, the angels who wrote nothing at all were standing beside the brethren who knowingly entertained voluntary distractions.

"The devout words which the lips pronounce awaken devotion in the heart," says the Angelic Doctor. For this very reason the Lord has taught us to use vocal prayer in order that the heart within may desire what the lips externally express. In regard to the words of David: "I have cried to the Lord with my voice" (Ps. 141:2), St. Augustine writes: "Many call upon the Lord, but not with their voice; that is to say, they call on the Lord not with the voice of the soul, but with the voice of the body. Call with your thoughts, call with your heart, and then the Lord will certainly hear you."

ASPIRATIONS

The easiest means of practicing vocal prayer consists in uttering fervent aspirations. These pious outpourings of the heart need not be restricted to any particular place or time. They are in order at all times and in all places, at work, at meals, at recreation, at home or away from home. They may take the form of acts of desire, conformity, love, oblation, or self-denial; they may be acts of petition, thanksgiving, humility, confidence and the like. The Saints of God placed greater value on these little prayers than on long devotions because the former are more calculated to keep us in the presence of God.

St. John Chrysostom says that he who frequently utters aspirations closes the door against Satan and prevents his constant annoyance with wicked thoughts. It is by acts of love, conformity and self-oblation, together with the invocation of the holy names of Jesus and Mary, that we give the greatest pleasure to God. One who loves, thinks constantly of the object of his love. A soul that loves God will therefore always think of Him and seek occasions, by fervent sighs and aspirations, to manifest her love. Be careful on all occasions, alone as well as in company, to say frequently to your heavenly Bridegroom: "O my God, I desire only Thee and nothing else"; or, "I give myself wholly to Thee; I desire what Thou desirest; do with me according to Thy good pleasure." These few words alone are enough: "My God, I love Thee"; or "My Love, my All!" You may also, without uttering a word, raise your eyes to Heaven or cast a loving glance at the tabernacle or the crucifix. These silent acts are especially to be recommended because they require no effort, they can more frequently be made, and are often attended with greater fervor than other aspirations. The best acts of love, of course, are those that well up from the depth of the heart at the impulse of the Holy Ghost.

The perfection of divine love consists in the union of our will with the Will of God. Therefore, we may not desire anything but that which God desires. If we do His holy will, no matter to what station in life the Lord may call us, we shall surely arrive at sanctity. It will be profitable, then, to select choice passages from Holy Scripture and to repeat them often in order to foster a union of our will with the Divine. For example, say often with the Apostle: "Lord, what wilt thou have me to do?" (Acts 9:6). In contradictions and afflictions of body and soul, say with our Blessed Redeemer: "My God and my Father, be it done to me as thou wilt."

(Matt. 11:26). "Thy will be done on earth as it is in Heaven." The Lord recommended to St. Catherine of Genoa, every time she said the Our Father, to pay particular attention to these words: "Thy will be done," and to beg for the grace to fulfill the Will of God as perfectly as the Saints in Heaven.

THE HOLY NAMES

Among all aspirations and prayers, the invocation of the holy names of Jesus, Mary and Joseph should have the first place. All that we love and desire and hope to possess is summed up in these beautiful names. The holy name of Jesus fills us with consolation, for when we invoke Him who bears it we find comfort in all our troubles. The name of Jesus is called by the Holy Ghost "oil poured out." (Cant. 1:2). And rightly so; for as oil serves as light, as food and as medicine, the holy name, according to St. Bernard, is a light; by this most sacred name we are happy children of the true light, i.e., faith in the true Church of God. The holy name is food for the nourishment of our souls, for it strengthens the faithful and affords them peace and consolation in the midst of the misery and persecutions of this world. Finally, the holy name is medicine for him who invokes it. "When the light of this name appears," says St. Bernard, "the clouds are dispersed and the heavens remain serene. When the soul is tossed about by the storms of trouble and sorrow, she needs but to call on the name of Jesus, and the storm will subside and calm will be restored. Should you have the misfortune to fall into sin and grow diffident of pardon, invoke the sacred names, and hope of forgiveness will revive in your soul."

St. Peter tells us that "there is no other name under heaven given to men, whereby we must be saved." (Acts 4:12). Jesus Christ has not saved us only once; He is continually saving us by His merits, when in accordance with His promise, He frees us from the danger of sin as often as we invoke His holy name. "Whatsoever you shall ask the Father in my name, that will I do." (John 14:13). Therefore St. Paul exhorts us not to neglect this great means of salvation, assuring us that "whosoever shall call upon the name of the Lord, shall be saved." (Rom. 10:13).

With the holy name of Jesus we must unite the beautiful name of Mary. The name of Mary, like that of Jesus, is a name from Heaven above, and it is so powerful that all Hell trembles when it is pronounced. At the same time, it is a name of exceeding sweetness because it denotes that exalted Queen who is at once the Mother of God and our mother, a mother of mercy, a mother of beautiful love.

As breath is a sign of life, says St. Germanus, the frequent invocation of the name of Mary is a sign that the grace of God is within us or will very soon be there. The holy name of Mary has particular efficacy in overcoming temptations against holy purity. "Happy is he," says St. Bonaventure, "who loves thy holy name, O Mary! Thy name is a glorious and wonderful name; they who invoke thy powerful name at the hour of death have nothing to fear from the assaults of Hell."

Finally, it has always been the laudable practice of devout Christians to unite with the names of Our Lord and His holy Mother the beautiful name of St. Joseph. If the King of Heaven and earth conferred on him the honor of being the foster father of His Beloved Son and the protector of the holy and Immaculate Mother, surely it behooves us to honor him and invoke his powerful intercession. St. Teresa says that she never remembers to have sought his aid in vain. "Jesus, Mary and Joseph, I give you my heart and my soul; Jesus, Mary and Joseph, assist me in my last agony; Jesus, Mary and Joseph, may I breathe forth my soul in peace with you."

MENTAL PRAYER OR MEDITATION

Our Divine Redeemer had no need, as St. Ambrose says, to retire to a lonely place to pray; for as His blessed soul was constantly in the presence of His heavenly Father, in every place and in all circumstances He thought of Him and continually interceded for us. Nevertheless, as St. Matthew relates, "Having dismissed the multitude he went into a mountain alone to pray. And when it was evening he was there alone." (Matt. 14:23). He did this to teach us the necessity of interior prayer or meditation.

The eternal truths are spiritual things; they cannot be seen with the bodily eyes, but only with the eyes of the soul, that is to say, by reflection and meditation. It is for want of reflection that, as the Holy Ghost says, "all the land is made desolate because there is none that considereth in the heart." (Jer. 12:11). Hence the exhortation of Our Lord: "Let your loins be girt and lamps burning in your hands." (Luke 12:35). These lamps, says St. Bonaventure, are devout meditations, for during interior prayer the Lord speaks to us and enlightens us. "Thy word is a lamp to my feet and a light to my paths." (Ps. 118:105).

St. Bernard compares mental prayer to a mirror, and the comparison is very apt; for if you happen to have a speck of dirt on the face and you come before a looking glass, you see the dirt at once and remove it. Had you not looked in the mirror, you would not have thought of the dirt nor washed it away. So it is with mental prayer: While at meditation we are standing, as it were, before a mirror of the soul. It is then we recognize our faults and the danger we are in, and accordingly we take measures to rid ourselves of the faults and to escape from the danger that threatens us. St. Teresa once wrote to the Bishop of Osma: "Although we appear to have no imperfections, we discover that we have very many when God opens the eyes of the soul, as He does in meditation." "He," says St. Bernard, "who does not meditate will scarcely ever perceive his faults, and as a result will have no horror of them."

Without meditation or mental prayer we are lacking in strength to resist the assaults of the enemies of our soul and to practice the Christian virtues. Meditation affects the soul as fire does iron. If iron is cold, it is very hard and cannot be worked without great difficulty. But put it in the fire, and at once it softens and easily yields to the efforts of the blacksmith. In order to observe the commandments and counsels of God, we have need of a pliable, that is to say, a docile heart, a heart that will easily receive the impressions of heavenly inspirations and as readily respond. It was for such a heart that Solomon prayed: "Give to thy servant, O Lord, an understanding heart, to discern between good and evil. And the word was pleasing to the Lord that Solomon had asked such a thing." (3 Kgs. 3:9–10).

In consequence of sin our heart is by nature a hard and obstinate heart, given to pleasures of sense and opposed to the law of the spirit. Therefore the Apostle complains: "I see another law in my members, fighting against the law of my mind, and captivating me in the law of sin, that is in my members." (Rom. 7:23). But under the influence of grace which we receive in meditation, the heart soon grows docile; the sight of God's goodness and mercy and the wondrous proofs of His love serve to inflame our hearts, and we listen with joy to the voice of our Lord and Master. St. Bernard, when writing to Pope Eugene III, begs him never to omit meditation, though many and weighty affairs may claim his time and attention.

NECESSITY OF MENTAL PRAYER

Without mental prayer we shall never practice the prayer of petition as we ought, and this prayer of petition is absolutely necessary for eternal salvation. "Pray without ceasing," says the Apostle. (1 Thess. 5:17). We are all poor beggars, as David once said of himself: "I am a beggar and poor." (Ps. 39:18). Now, the only hope of the poor is to ask alms from the rich. In our spiritual poverty our only recourse is to beg God, by prayer, for the graces of which we stand in need. St. John Chrysostom says: "Without prayer it is absolutely impossible to lead a virtuous life." Whence the universal depravity of morals, asks the learned Bishop Abelly, if not from the neglect of prayer? As we have seen before, the absence of meditation makes us blind to our own condition and needs; hence we are led to neglect the prayer of petition. A great servant of God once said: "Meditation and sin cannot exist together"; and experience teaches that those who are zealous in the practice of meditation rarely, if ever, fall into God's displeasure. A soul that loves meditation, says the Royal Psalmist, is like a tree that is planted by the running waters; it bringeth forth fruit in due season, and all its actions are meritorious before God. (Ps. 1:2–3).

THE METHOD OF ST. ALPHONSUS

For the exercise of mental prayer it is well to follow some approved method. The method of St. Alphonsus is a very commendable one because it is both simple and practical. He divides the meditation into three parts: the preparation, the consideration and the conclusion. With regard to the preparation he says: Endeavor to dispose both soul and body for this important exercise. Dismiss all distracting thoughts and say what St. Bernard said on entering a church: "Remain here, all you earthly and distracting thoughts. I may have leisure for you after meditation." Recite briefly an act of faith in the presence of God, together with profound adoration of His infinite Majesty. Humbly ask pardon for your past offenses, and beg for light and grace to make your meditation well. Recommend yourself to the Blessed Virgin, St. Joseph, your Guardian Angel and your holy patrons. These acts must be very fervent but brief, so as to proceed at once with the consideration. For the meditation proper it is good to use a book, at least in the beginning, so as to hold the attention on the subject for consideration. Pause from time to time when you are particularly impressed in order that, like the bee, you may extract the honey from the flower, or like the dove, take a drink and then look up to Heaven before taking another.

The importance of mental prayer, however, consists not so much in the consideration as in the affections, petitions, and resolutions which must accompany it. The consideration may be likened to a needle, and the affections, petitions and resolutions are the thread of gold that follows it. The affections will consist of short and fervent acts of humility, confidence and gratitude; frequently repeat aspirations of love and contrition, for these are the links of the golden chain that unites the soul to God. One act of perfect love is sufficient to obtain the pardon of all your sins. "Charity covereth a multitude of sins," says St. Peter (1 Ptr. 4:8). St. Thomas teaches that every act of love merits a new degree of glory. Perhaps the most important part of the meditation is the petitions which you address to God. The Lord loves to be importuned; and, therefore, never weary asking Him for light and grace, for conformity to His holy Will and perseverance in good; above all things, beg Him earnestly to grant you His holy love. With love, says St. Francis de Sales, we receive all other graces.

Before the Venerable Father Segneri studied theology, he contented himself while at meditation with considerations and affections; but finally, says he himself, "God opened my eyes and from that time on I devoted myself to petitions, and if there is aught of good in me now I owe it to this beautiful custom." Follow the example of this holy man and ask in the name of Jesus Christ for all the graces you need, for God has promised to hear and answer your prayers: "Amen, amen, I say to you: if you ask the Father anything in my name he will give it you." (John 16:23). At the end of meditation proper it is very useful to make a special resolution to avoid some particular fault, or to be more zealous in the practice of a particular virtue. This resolution must be repeated until the desired end is attained. Outside the time of meditation we must endeavor to profit by the opportunities afforded to carry out our resolutions.

The conclusion of the meditation consists in the following acts: First, thank God for the enlightenment you have received; secondly, express your determination to carry out the resolutions you have made; thirdly, ask the heavenly Father, for the love of Jesus and Mary, to grant you the grace to be faithful to your resolutions.

It is a beautiful custom, at the end of meditation, to recommend to God the souls in Purgatory and all poor sinners. "Nothing," says St. John Chrysostom, "proves our love for Jesus Christ better than the zeal we have to pray for our brethren." St. Francis de Sales counsels us to gather a little spiritual nosegay from the meditation and to enjoy its perfume through the day. He wishes to say that we should select one or two thoughts that have impressed us in the morning meditation, and recall them frequently during the day to reanimate our fervor and to preserve the fruit of the morning meditation.

If you are annoyed by distractions during mental prayer, recall to mind the words of St. Francis de Sales: "If you are occupied during the whole meditation in fighting distractions and temptations you will have made a good meditation. The Lord looks to the good intention we have and the effort we make, and these He rewards." In another place he says: "In prayer we must not seek the delights of God, but the God of delights." "Ask and it shall be given you; seek and you shall find; knock and it shall be opened to you." (Matt. 7:7). "Speak, Lord, for thy servant heareth." (1 Kgs. 3:9).

Chapter XII

Self-Denial and Love of the Cross

"If any man will come after me, let him deny himself and take up his cross and follow me."—Matt. 16:24

The love which our Divine Master Jesus entertained for the cross was so great that He embraced it from the first moment of His Incarnation. The will of His heavenly Father had decreed that His life on earth should be the way of the cross; accordingly, He began His sorrowful journey to Calvary's Mount the very moment that "the Word was made flesh and dwelt amongst us." If we desire to be made conformable to the image of the Word Incarnate, we must needs love God's will and carry our cross with patience and resignation. The cross is the nuptial couch to which our Saviour invites us. "He that taketh not up his cross and followeth me is not worthy of me." (Matt. 10:38). Hand in hand with the love of the cross is the virtue of self-denial, for he who is attached to the comforts of life or to himself lacks courage to walk in the blood-stained footsteps of the suffering Saviour.

"Patience hath a perfect work," says the Apostle (James 1:4), for by patience in bearing the crosses of life we make a perfect sacrifice to God. With resignation to His holy will we embrace the cross which He sends us and esteem it more highly even than one of our own choosing.

Patience, says the Wise Man, is to be preferred to the courage of the hero: "The patient man is better than the valiant: and he that ruleth his spirit, than he that taketh cities." (Prov. 16:32). Many a man will display great courage in undertaking and bringing to completion some pious work; but he may not have patience enough to bear with the little annoyances and contradictions he encounters. For such a one it were better to be steadfast in patient suffering than courageous in great undertakings. We are in this world to gain merit; therefore this earth is not a place of rest, but of work and suffering. Merits are not gained by repose and rest, but by labor and constant effort. All men must suffer, the just as well as the sinner. One is lacking in this, another is deprived of that. This man is noble but not wealthy; that man is rich but has no claim to nobility, while still another is both noble and rich, but he has lost his health. In a word we all have something to endure, be we high or low, rich or poor, learned or unlearned, sinners or saints.

PEACE OF HEART

Accordingly, we can enjoy true peace of heart only when we carry our cross with patience and resignation. The Holy Ghost warns us not to act as irrational animals which become enraged when they cannot gratify their desires: "Do not become like the horse and the mule who have no understanding." (Ps. 31:9). Of what use is it to be impatient in trouble and contradictions? We only increase our burden thereby. The two thieves who were crucified with our Blessed Redeemer were suffering similar torments; but the good thief was saved because he bore them with patience, while the bad thief was eternally lost because he suffered impatiently and rebelled. The same trial, says St. Augustine, leads the good to glory because they suffer with patience and resignation, but the wicked to eternal destruction from a want of patience and conformity to God's will.

When we try to avoid a cross that the Lord has sent us, we often meet with another, and a much heavier one. "They that fear the hoary frost," says Job, "the snow shall fall upon them." (6:16). Only take this cross from me, you say; any other I am willing to bear. Ah yes, but that other cross may be heavier still and you have little or no merit for carrying it. Therefore embrace the cross that God sends you, no matter what it may be; it is lighter and more meritorious than any other, for you are doing God's will and not your own.

St. Augustine says the whole life of a Christian must be one perpetual cross. This is especially true of those who are striving after perfection. St. Gregory Nazianzen says that "with great and generous souls riches consist in poverty, honor in contempt, and joy in the absence of all earthly pleasures." When asked who it is that really strives after perfection, St. John Climacus replied: "He who constantly does violence to himself." And when will the necessity of doing violence to oneself cease? Only when life is at an end, for St. Prosper says: "The struggle will be over only when we are certain of the victory, that is, when we have entered the Kingdom of Heaven."

VALUE OF SUFFERING

If you are forced to acknowledge, dear Christian reader, that you have offended your God, and you wish at the same time to sanctify your immortal soul, you should rejoice when God sends you suffering. "Sin," says St. John Chrysostom, "is an ulcer of the soul; if suffering does not come to remove the corrupted matter the soul will be lost." When God gives you something to suffer, says St. Augustine, He acts as a physician, and the suffering He sends is not a punishment but a remedy. "Whom the Lord loveth, he chastiseth, and he scourgeth every son whom he receiveth." (Heb. 12:6). "If everything goes well," says St. Augustine, "acknowledge the Father who caresses you; if you have suffering to endure, acknowledge the Father who chastises you." "Hasten, O Lord," cries St. Bonaventure, "hasten and wound Thy servants with the wounds of love and salvation, that we may not succumb to the wounds of anger and eternal death." "God is never more angry," says St. Bernard, "than when He is not angry with the sinner and fails to punish him."

But suffering is not only an excellent means of atoning for past sins, it is also an abundant source of merit. "When there is question of winning Heaven," says St. Joseph Calasanctius, "all pains must be regarded as trifling and insignificant." The Apostle had said long before: "For I reckon that the sufferings of this time are not worthy to be compared with the glory to come that shall be revealed in us." (Rom. 8:18). It would be little if we had to endure all the sufferings of this world for one moment of the joys of Heaven. How much more, therefore, ought we to bear patiently every cross that God sends us when we know that the brief suffering of this life will be followed by the eternal happiness of the next. "For that which is at present momentary and light of our tribulation worketh for us above measure exceedingly an eternal weight of glory." (2 Cor. 4:17). The greater our merits here, the greater our glory hereafter. Hence St. James says: "Blessed is the man that endureth temptation; for when he hath been proved, he shall receive the crown of life which God hath promised to them that love him." (James 1:12).

Animated with this thought St. Agapitus, a youth of fifteen years, displayed most admirable heroism while suffering martyrdom. When the tyrant had burning coals placed on his head, the youthful martyr cried out: "It matters very little indeed that this head is burned with coals on earth, as long as it will be crowned with glory in Heaven." It was this same thought that prompted holy Job to say: "If we have received good things at the hand of the Lord, why should we not receive evil?" (Job 2:10). The good that I expect, says St. Francis de Sales, is so exceeding great that every pain becomes for me a pleasure: "In view of all I hope to gain, my labors here have naught of pain."

A PROOF OF LOVE

Suffering is the touchstone of love. There are many, says the Wise Man, who are friends in the time of prosperity—but with the advent of adversity they disappear. "For there is a friend for his own occasion, and he will not abide in the day of thy trouble." (Ecclus. 6:8). But the surest proof of genuine love is shown by the man who voluntarily suffers for his friend. Consequently, we offer a most agreeable sacrifice to God when we willingly embrace the cross that He sends. "Love is patient," says St. Paul, "it beareth all things." (1 Cor. 13:4, 7). It patiently carries the external as well as the internal cross: for example, the loss of health, of fortune, of honor, of relatives and friends; anguish, temptations, pains and spiritual aridity. By patience virtue is tried. On this account such stress is laid, in the lives of the Saints, on their patience in contradictions. The devil tempts us to try our patience. "Gold and silver are tried in the fire, but acceptable men in the furnace of humiliation." (Ecclus. 2:5). "Because thou wast acceptable to God, it was necessary that temptation should prove thee." (Tob. 12:13). When the Lord gives one an occasion of suffering much, says St. John Chrysostom, He shows a greater love for such a one than if He gave him the power to raise the dead to life; for when we work miracles we are debtors to God, but when we suffer patiently, God becomes so to say a debtor to us.

How is it possible to look at a crucifix and see a God who died in an ocean of sufferings and contempt, without bearing patiently for love of Him all the sufferings that God may choose to send us? St. Mary Magdalen de Pazzi once said: "Every pain, howsoever great, becomes sweet when we contemplate Jesus on the Cross." When the learned Justus Lipsius was enduring great suffering, one of the bystanders encouraged him to be patient by recalling the example of some pagan philosophers. The sufferer raised his eyes to the crucifix and said: "Here is true patience." He wished to say: the example of a God who suffered so much for love of us is sufficient incentive for us to suffer all pains for love of Him. "He who loves the Crucified," says St. Bernard, "loves suffering and contempt." When St. Eleazar was asked by his saintly spouse Delphina how he could bear so many insults from boorish men, without resentment, he replied: "You must not imagine that I am not sensitive to these insults; I feel them very keenly; but I turn to Jesus Crucified and continue to gaze upon Him until my mind is quiet, and a balm is laid upon my wounded feelings."

Whether we will it or no, we must all bear the sufferings that God's Providence has allotted to us. It is to our advantage, therefore, to suffer with merit, and that means to suffer with patience. Pray God earnestly for this precious gift, the grace to suffer the trials and tribulations of life with patience and conformity to His holy will. "To him who overcometh I will give a hidden manna." (Apoc. 2:17). Patience is to be exercised above all during sickness. Character and disposition are revealed by this infallible touchstone and shown to be genuine gold or sham.

Many people are cheerful, patient and devout as long as they enjoy good health; but as soon as they are visited by sickness, they commit innumerable faults; they grow impatient toward everyone around them and find fault with the care or want of care that is shown them; they complain of every little pain they suffer and allow their imagination to increase their troubles.

"If we only knew what a treasure we possess in hidden sufferings," said St. Vincent de Paul, "we would accept them as gladly as the greatest benefits." St. Vincent himself suffered without complaint the most violent pains, which often left him without rest both day and night; and yet he was cheerful, as though he had nothing whatever to endure. Oh, how edifying it is at the time of suffering to preserve a cheerful peace and resignation!

Whenever St. Francis de Sales was ill, he simply stated the matter to the physician and then obeyed him exactly, taking the medicines prescribed, however repugnant they might be. After this he remained perfectly quiet and never complained of what he had to suffer. "Learn to suffer for the love of God," says St. Teresa, "and don't be anxious for everyone to find it out." By a special grace of God the saintly Father Louis de Ponte was permitted one Good Friday to suffer a special pain in every part of his body. This he told to one of his friends, but he had scarcely done so when he regretted it to such an extent that he made a vow never after to tell others what he had to suffer. I say it was "by a special grace" that he suffered, for the Saints accept sufferings and tribulations as manifestations of God's favor.

A very devout woman lay grievously sick and was tortured with violent pains; they placed a crucifix in her hands and told her to pray to the Lord to free her from suffering. "How can you counsel me," she said, "to come down from the cross of suffering while I hold my Crucified Saviour in my hands? I will gladly suffer for love of Him who endured greater torments for love of me."

This is what Our Lord said one day to St. Teresa when she was sick and suffered great pain. He appeared to her covered with wounds and spoke to her as follows: "Look at these wounds, My daughter; your pains will never be as great as Mine." This led the Saint ever afterward to say: "When I think of Our Lord, who was so innocent and yet suffered so much, I cannot see how I can complain of my ailments." "Many," says Salvian, "would never have reached sanctity had they enjoyed good health." And it seems very true, for if you read the lives of the Saints you will be astonished at the sufferings so many of them had to endure. These sufferings were stepping-stones to great holiness and intimate union with God.

I complain, not because I am sick, you will say, but because I cannot go to church, and receive Holy Communion and pray; moreover I am a burden to others.

But tell me, why do you wish to go to church and to receive Holy Communion? Is it not to please God? Very well, but now if it is more pleasing to God that you remain away from church and Holy Communion, and suffer instead on a bed of pain, what reason have you to be disturbed? Listen to what Venerable John of Avila wrote one day to a priest who was very ill: "My friend, do not think now of what you would do if you were well, but be content to remain sick as long as it pleases God. If you are seeking the will of God, what matters it whether you are sick or well?" St. Francis de Sales maintained that we can serve God better by suffering than by laboring.

TO SUFFER IS TO PRAY

You say you cannot pray? Why not? I will grant that you cannot meditate for any length of time, but what prevents you from turning your eyes to Jesus Crucified and offering Him the sufferings you must endure. The best prayer you can say is to resign yourself to the will of God in the midst of your sufferings, uniting your pains to the pains of Jesus Christ and offering them as a sacrifice to God. It was thus St. Vincent de Paul acted when he was mortally ill. He placed himself in the presence of God, and from time to time made an act of love, of confidence, of gratitude or of resignation, especially when his pains became very violent. St. Francis de Sales said: "Sufferings in themselves are very abhorrent to our inclinations; but when considered with reference to the will of God they cause us joy and pleasure." And finally you say you are a burden to others. It must be evident to all that your helpless condition is not of your own choosing, but is simply in accordance with the will of God. Therefore the complaints you make cannot proceed from the love of God, but are the expressions of self-love; we would like to serve the Lord, but in our own way, and not as He desires.

Father Balthasar Alvarez was one day permitted to see the glory that God had prepared for a religious as the reward of her patient endurance of suffering, and he asserted that this holy person had gained more merit in eight months of suffering than other zealous religious had gained in several years. While St. Ludwina was suffering great pain she entertained the desire to die a martyr's death. One day when she experienced a particular yearning for this grace, she saw a brilliant but unfinished crown and she was given to understand that this crown was intended for her. Desiring the crown to be perfectly finished, she prayed God to increase her sufferings. The Lord heard her prayer. Some brutal soldiers entered and, after insulting her with the vilest epithets, cruelly beat her. An angel at once appeared with the beautiful crown completed and said that her last sufferings added to the crown the jewels which had been wanting. When the angel had finished speaking, the virgin expired.

Another opportunity is afforded us for the practice of patience by the persecutions to which we are sometimes exposed. "I have done nothing to deserve these insults and this persecution," you may say; "why should I have to endure them?" But do you remember what Our Lord said to St. Peter the Martyr when the Saint complained that he was imprisoned unjustly? "O Lord, what evil have I done that I should suffer this persecution?" Our Saviour made answer: "And what evil have I done that I should be nailed to this Cross?"

A SOURCE OF MERIT

In the writings of St. Teresa we find these remarkable words: "He who strives after perfection must be careful never to say: someone has done me a wrong. If you are willing to carry no other cross but that which you deserve, you have no claim to perfection." When

St. Philip Neri lived near the church of St. Jerome in Rome, he suffered continually from the insults and annoyances of the evil-minded men of the neighborhood, and this for a period of 30 years. When finally he was urged by his spiritual sons to leave his old abode and live in a new monastery recently founded, he refused to do so, and could be prevailed upon only by an express command of the Holy Father.

The Saints have all had to suffer persecution of some kind. St. Basil was accused of heresy before Pope Damasus. St. Cyril of Alexandria was condemned by a council of 40 bishops and deprived of this episcopal see. St. Athanasius was accused of witchcraft, and St. Chrysostom of immorality. When more than 100 years old, St. Romuald was charged with a heinous crime, and they said he deserved to be burnt alive. And so on, from the first to the last in the calendar of the Saints of God. Indeed it could not be otherwise, for as the Apostle says: "All they that will live godly in Christ Jesus shall suffer persecution." (2 Tim. 3:12).

If therefore, says St. Augustine, you do not care to suffer persecution, there is reason to fear that you have not begun to follow Jesus Christ. Who was holier than Our Lord and God? And yet He was persecuted to such an extent that He died on a cruel cross, the victim of calumny and injustice. How can we complain when we see our Master and Model before us! "If you do not believe my words, believe my works." (John 10:38). "They have dug my hands and feet; they have numbered all my bones." (Ps. 21:17–18).

SPIRITUAL ARIDITY

There is a great need of patience in bearing the cross of spiritual abandonment, for it is one of the hardest trials that a soul who loves God can endure. When a devout person is enjoying spiritual consolations, all manner of external trials are unable to disturb him. On the contrary, they only seem to increase the joy of his heart as they afford him an opportunity to offer his sufferings to the Lord and thus become more closely united to Him. But to experience no devotion, no zeal, no holy desires, but on the contrary only coldness and dryness at prayer and at Holy Communion is the most bitter pain that a soul that loves God can endure. St. Teresa says that such a soul gives the surest proof of her love when, without any apparent incentive, and even in spite of interior repugnance and agony of soul, she continues patiently on her way. "By aridity of spirit and temptations," says the Saint, "the Lord proves those whom

He loves." When St. Angela of Foligno was once suffering from this spiritual dryness, she complained to the Lord that He had abandoned her. "No, My daughter," replied the Lord, "I love you now more than before, and regard you as more closely united to Me than ever."

It is a delusion, says St. Francis de Sales, to judge piety according to the measure of consolations that we experience in the service of God. True piety, he continues, consists in the determined will to do all that is pleasing to God. By means of spiritual aridity, God unites Himself intimately with the souls He loves in an especial manner. What hinders us from being truly united to God is attachment to our inordinate inclinations. When God, therefore, desires to lead a soul to His perfect love, He endeavors first to free her from all attachment to created things. To this end He deprives her little by little of earthly goods such as riches, honors, relatives, bodily health and so forth. Then follow contradictions and humiliations of every sort. These are so many means that the Lord makes use of to divest the soul of all attachments to creatures and to self.

In the beginning of the soul's conversion, God often gives her a flood of consolations. In consequence of this, the soul is gradually weaned from attachment to creatures and gives herself to God; but not as yet in a perfect manner, for she acts more for the sake of the consolations of God than for the God of consolations, as St. Francis de Sales so beautifully says. It is a common fault of our fallen nature that in everything we do, we seek our own gratification. The love of God and Christian perfection do not consist in sweet feelings and sensible consolations, but in overcoming our self-love and in fulfilling the Will of God. In the lives of God's greatest servants and saints we see the milk of consolations give place to the more substantial food of afflictions; and this it is that enables them to bear the burden of the cross on their journey to Calvary's Mount. To a very holy person who suffered from spiritual aridity St. John of the Cross wrote as follows: "Never were you in a better condition than now, because you were never so humbled and so detached from the world, and never did you recognize your misery so well, as at this very moment. Never were you so indifferent about yourself and never did you seek yourself less."

Oh, how dear to the heart of God are acts of confidence and resignation in the midst of the darkness of spiritual aridity. Let us, therefore, place our unbounded trust in God, who, as St. Teresa says, loves us more than we love ourselves.

THE HOUR OF DEATH

When the hour of death is at hand it is above all necessary to be resigned to the Will of God. Our life on earth is a continued storm in which we are in constant danger of perishing. St. Aloysius Gonzaga, who died in the bloom of youth, accepted death with joy, saying: "I am now, I hope, in the grace of God; I do not know what may happen to me later; therefore I gladly accept death at this moment, if it pleases God to call me out of this life."

But then you will say: Aloysius was a saint, and I am a sinner. Listen to what the Venerable John of Avila says: "If our soul is only in a moderately good condition, we should desire death, in order to escape the danger of losing the grace of God." But you may say: I have not yet gained any merit for my soul; I would like to live a little longer and do some good before I die. Who gives you the assurance that if your life is prolonged you will not be even worse than before, and perhaps be eternally lost? "Why do you desire to live," says St. Bernard, "when the longer we live, the more we sin?" If we truly love God we must have a desire to see Him face to face in Heaven and love Him with an endless, unchangeable love. But death must open the gates to eternal life, and therefore St. Augustine, aglow with love for his God, cried out: "O Lord, permit me to die that I may come to see Thee face to face and enjoy Thee forever 'where eye hath not seen, nor ear heard, neither hath it entered into the heart of man what things God hath prepared for them that love him.'" (1 Cor. 2:9).